MMX

a photography of Britain

———

a documentary work

www.inspirita.org

Inspirita, 12 Vale Road, Bowdon, Cheshire, UK WA14 3AQ
www.inspirita.org

ISBN 9 781905 553808

◄ inspirita ►

I am a camera
I see things
I see things as they are

I am not a large expensive 'I am the photographer' camera
I can slip out of a woman's handbag or a gentleman's pocket
in an instant and no one would ever notice me on the street

I do not have a social or cultural identity
I do not have political or religious beliefs
I do not seek power or wealth or pleasure
I do not drink or smoke or take drugs
I am immune to pampering or harassment
I do not have inexplicable mood swings
I am always the same at every point in time

whether a person is shining with virtuosity
or entombed in the darkest human place

I look at everything in exactly the same way

that is my nature

I am a camera
I see things
I see things as they are

the camera is the buddha

Holiday Inn   Salisbury, Wiltshire   New Year's Eve

january

The Presence Of The Moon   Avebury, Wiltshire   Dawn, New Year

The Presence Of the Sun   Avebury, Wiltshire   Dawn, New Year

The Presence Of the Earth   Avebury, Wiltshire   Dawn, New Year

The outstanding pre-historic ceremonial site of Europe, the miracle of Stonehenge, dating back four and a half thousand years to c. 2,500 BC.

It speaks to us of a reality of awe and worship - a reality that predates modern law, religion, society and culture.

Its sacred message still beats deep within the heart of Britain.

The Presence Of The Sacred   Stonehenge, Wiltshire   New Year's Day

The Neolithic era (4,000-2,000 BC) saw the gradual transition from the original migrant hunter gatherer populations to a more settled way of life.   Societies divided into differing groups of farmers, artisans and leaders.

Forests were cleared to provide room for cereal cultivation and the domestication of animal herds.   Native cattle and pigs were reared whilst sheep and goats were introduced from the continent, together with wheat and barley.   Cave occupation was common at this time.

The Presence Of The Human   Stonehenge, Wiltshire   New Year's Day

New Year Posh   West Lavington Down, Wiltshire   New Year's Day

The story goes that in the colonial era the more well-to-do passengers on ships travelling between England and India used to have POSH written against their bookings, standing for 'Port Out, Starboard Home', indicating the more desirable cabins, on the shady side of the ship.

Unfortunately, this story did not make its appearance until the 1930s, by which time the term had already been in use for some twenty years. Added to this, the word does not appear to have been recorded in the form 'P.O.S.H.', which would be expected if it had started life as an abbreviation.

Despite exhaustive enquiries, interviews with former travellers and inspection of shipping company documents, researchers for the 20-volume historical Oxford English Dictionary have found no supporting evidence for this explanation of the origins of posh.
Oxford Dictionaries   2010

Posh may derive from the late 19th century slang term posh meaning 'dandy, swell', possibly stemming from the early 19th-century slang term posh 'halfpenny', hence broadly 'money', perhaps ultimately from the Romany word posh 'half'.
Word-Origins   2010

Offering typically generous portions,
a traditional New Year 'nosh-up' at a British pub.
Nosh - London slang thought to have spun off the
East End Yiddish word for a snack, 'nashun'.

New Year Nosh   Chippenham, Wiltshire   New Year's Day

The First Snow   Hawes, Wensleydale, N. Yorkshire   Jan 03

The First Monday   London Bridge, London   Jan 04

Commute   First Monday, London   Jan 04

City   First Monday, London   Jan 04

Swiss Re   City of London   Jan 04

Stock Exchange   City of London   Jan 04

Lloyds   City of London   Jan 04

Bank of England   City of London   Jan 04

The Young   Repatriation, Wootton Bassett, Wiltshire   Jan 05

The Veterans   Repatriation, Wootton Bassett, Wiltshire   Jan 05

Sapper David Watson - 33 Engineer Regiment - Age 23

Sadly died of wounds sustained in an explosion near Patrol Base
Blenheim in the Sangin region of Helmand Province,
caused by an IED on Thursday December 31, 2009.

Rifleman Aidan Powell - 3rd Battalion The Rifles - Age 19

Tragically killed as a result of an explosion near
forward operating Base Zeebrugge, in the Kajaki area
of Helmand Province, on the afternoon of 28 Dec 2009.
He had been on patrol when an IED detonated.

The Fallen   Repatriation, Wootton Bassett, Wiltshire   Jan 05

White Out   British Isles   Jan 06

A rare occurrence, a Britain completely covered in snow, as shown in this NASA pic.

After many years of mild winters, the winter of 2010 came as something of a shock.

It turned out to be the coldest, longest winter since 1963, and in Scotland since 1947.

Winter Oak   Dunham Massey, Cheshire   Jan 07

Up Helly Aa   Lerwick, Shetland Isles   Jan 26

In the annual Up Helly Aa festival, the Shetland Islanders celebrate their Nordic roots with a torchlit procession and a ceremonial burning of a Viking long boat.

Conquered by Vikings in the 8th and 9th centuries, the Shetland & Orkney Isles were Norse until 1468 when, in exchange for 58,000 Rhenish guilders in a dowry deal, they were transferred to Scotland by King Christian 1 of Denmark & Norway on the occasion of his daughter's, Prince Magrethe's marriage to James III of Scotland.

In the dowry agreement and never subsequently honoured, there was a buy back clause for the Kings of Norway to be able to redeem Shetland and Orkney for 210 kgs of gold, approx. $9 million dollars at 2010 values.

(Photographic conditions were bedevilled by an incessant wind blown drizzle)

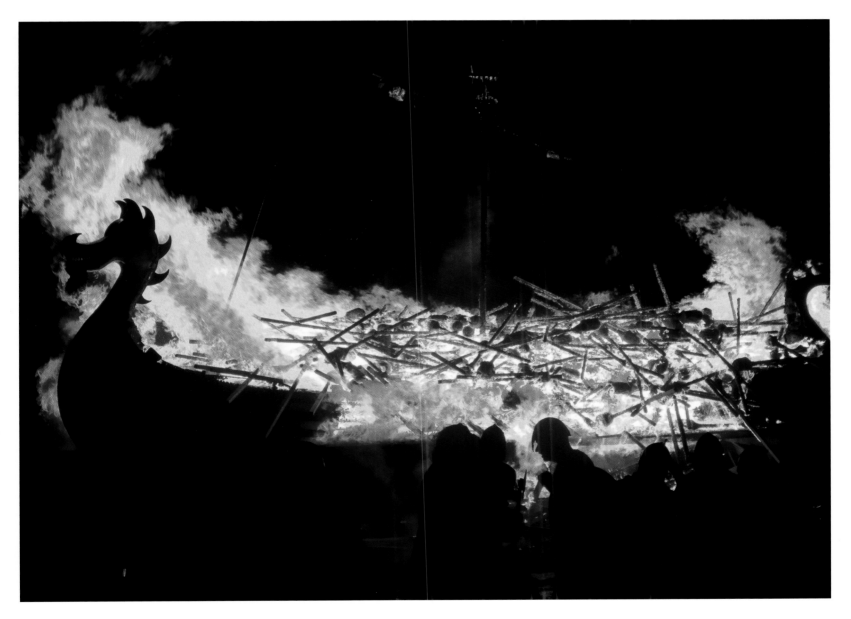

Up Helly Aa   Lerwick, Shetland Isles   Jan 26

Hurled aboard with great gusto and much chanting, the torches from the procession set the Viking long boat spectacularly ablaze.

The relevance of this otherwise awesome act of fealty to the Nordic Gods cannot be entirely separated from the monumental drinking bout that follows on throughout the night. Immense hangovers are not uncommon the next day.

Whiteness Voe   Mainland, Shetland Isles   Jan 27

In From The Cold   Fraserburgh, Aberdeenshire   Jan 27

Morning Fish Market   Fraserburgh, Aberdeenshire   Jan 28

The trawler fleet out of Fraserburgh accounts for 50% of the North East fleet and is the largest shellfish port in Europe. The North East fleet accounts for 13% of the total British catch.

Seriously affected by fishing quota restrictions, regularly abused by foreign fishing vessels, 'Employment In The Catching Sector' has declined by 39% since 1998, though levelling out and slightly increasing since 2003. (Scottish Government and DEFRA)

Fishing Fleet   Fraserburgh, Aberdeenshire   Jan 28

First Cut   Macduff Shipyards, Macduff, Aberdeenshire   Jan 28

Final Fit   Macduff Shipyards, Macduff, Aberdeenshire   Jan 28

The 174 tonne state of the art prawn/whitefish trawler 'Excel' nearing completion,
being readied for Caley Fisheries Ltd, out of Fraserburgh.

Dry Dock   Macduff Shipyards, Macduff   Aberdeenshire   Jan 28

Although Tony Blair had been re-elected as Prime Minister in the General Election of 2005, two years after the 2003 invasion of Iraq, and although the two Labour Party Conferences of Autumn 2003 & Autumn 2004 could have deposed him as Leader of the Labour Party, and although police and media personnel outside the Inquiry venue easily outnumbered protesters and although there had been four previous inquiries into pre-war intelligence, nevertheless the calling of Tony Blair before the Iraq Inquiry was a moment that had been keenly awaited by millions of people in Britain who felt, and still feel, bitterly betrayed and deeply shamed by the British role in the Iraq war. Those who protested the war and who had loved ones killed in action have been left agonisingly bereft.

In the event, in a typically polished 'Blairite' media savvy presentation, Tony Blair submitted an unyielding defence of his actions before the Inquiry.

Tony Blair Before The Iraq Inquiry   Westminster, London   Jan 29

The Execution Of King Charles I, January 30th, 1649   Whitehall, London   Jan 30

Resplendent on a charger at the southern end of Trafalgar square, King Charles I gazes regally down Whitehall to the place in front of the Banqueting House where, 361 years ago to the day, his head was severed from his body.

It is said that when he was beheaded a large groan went up throughout the crowd. One observer in the crowd described it as "such a groan by the thousands then present, as I never heard before and I desire I may never hear again." The King's execution shocked the whole of Europe.

For his role in the English Civil War, Charles I had been convicted of treason by a High Court of Justice set up by Parliament. Seven days after the execution, Parliament abolished the Monarchy, replacing it with a Council of State with Oliver Cromwell as its first Chairman. Seven weeks later, Parliament abolished the House of Lords as 'useless and dangerous to the people of England'.

Although the monarchy was reinstated in the Restoration Settlement of 1660 with not inconsiderable public support, nevertheless the notion of the Divine Right of Kings had been consigned to history. The era of a Constitutional Monarch without political power, and under the Rule of Law, had begun.

Chinese Witch Hazel   Bowdon, Cheshire   Feb 20

february

The Last Cast   Redcar, Teesside   Feb 19

The blast furnace glows for the last time.

Two hours later, the furnace was shut down,
ending 150 years of steel making on Teesside.

The Anglo Dutch firm Corus was bought by India's Tata steel in 2006 and the closure of the Redcar Cast Products factory with the loss of 1,700 jobs immediately called into question Tata's global strategy. Despite a long campaign to save or sell the plant, its blast furnace, its steel melt-slab shop, and one of its two coking ovens were shut down.

Although manufacturing now represents only one eighth of the UK economy, it still generates half its exports. Much of the Redcar slab was exported, so its mothballing worsens Britain's persistent, and worrying, trade deficit.

The good folk of Redcar knew what to do. In the General Election three months later, the Labour Party majority of 12,100 in the local constituency was overturned to a 5,200 majority for the Liberal Democrats.

The Steel Plant   Redcar, Teesside   Feb 19

With a centre span of 1,410 metres and a total length of 2,220 metres, the Humber Bridge was the longest single-span suspension bridge in the world for 16 years from 1981-1997. A huge project and a testament to British engineering, its construction lasted eight years from 1973-1981.

Due to the curvature of the earth, the towers, although both vertical, are not parallel, being 36 millimetres farther apart at the top than the bottom.

The Bridge   Hull, Humberside   Feb 19

The Deep   Hull   Feb 27

In Deep   The Deep, Hull   Feb 27

Skateboarders   Hull   Feb 27

Wannabes   Leicester   Feb 27

My Team   Walker Stadium, Leicester   Feb 27

The Away Fans   Walker Stadium, Leicester   Feb 27

Masjid Umar Mosque   Evington Road, Leicester   Feb 27

Since the war Leicester has experienced large scale immigration from across the world.
Immigrant groups today make up around 40% of Leicester's population, making it one
of the most ethnically diverse cities in the UK.

Many Polish servicemen, prevented from returning to their homeland after the war by the
communist regime, established a small community in Leicester. Economic migrants from
Ireland continued throughout the post war period and immigrants from India & Pakistan
began to arrive in the 1960s, their numbers boosted by Asians expelled from Kenya and
Uganda in the early 1970s In the 1990s, drawn by the city's free and easy atmosphere
and by its mosques, Dutch citizens of Somali origin settled. Since the 2004 enlargement
of the EEC, a significant number of East European migrants have settled in the city.

While some wards in the northeast of the city are more than 70% Asian, wards in the west
and south are over 70% white. The Commission For Racial Equality has estimated that
by 2011 Leicester would have approximately a 50% ethnic minority population, making it
the first city in Britain not to have a white British majority.

From midnight on 30 November 1967, due to President Kenyatta's project to "Africanise" his country, anyone who did not hold citizenship of Kenya would have to apply for an "entry certificate" to remain in the country, even if they had been born there. Foreigners could only hold a job until a Kenyan national could be found to replace them and many cities demanded that the government bans non-Kenyans from owning a shop or trading in municipal markets.

Many of the 200,000 Asians in Kenya knew they were no longer safe and opted to migrate to the UK under the then British Nationality Act of 1948, which permitted the 800 million subjects of the King in the British Empire to enter, live and work in the UK, without needing a visa.

In August 1972, following an alleged dream in which, he claimed, God had told him to expel them, Idi Amin, the notoriously brutal President of Uganda, gave Uganda's Asians, mostly Gujaratis of Indian origin, 90 days to leave the country.

Forty years later, an East African Asian family celebrates a wedding anniversary at a restaurant in Leicester.

East African Asian Family   Melton Road, Leicester   Feb 27

Hare Krishna

Evington Road, Leicester

Feb 27

Hare Krishna Hare Krishna
Krishna Krishna Hare Hare
Hare Rama Hare Rama
Rama Rama Hare Hare

The sixteen word Hare Krishna mantra derives from one of the Upanishads, ancient texts central to the Indian spiritual tradition.

It rose in importance from the 15th century onwards due to the Bhakti movement which asserted that the goal of life and one's original consciousness is the pure love of God. What is called ' Krishna consciousness' is not an artificial imposition on the mind. This consciousness is considered to be the original energy of the living entity.

Hare Rama   Evington Road, Leicester   Feb 27

The Hare Krishna people, who perform their duty to the universe through the medium of love and devotion.

The Lion of Knidos, Turkey, 250 BC   British Museum, London   March 24

march

Winter Bare   Caernarfon, N Wales   March 08

450 - 550 million years ago, the Cambrian Mountains of Wales were formed at the same time as most of the life forms that we see today first appeared on earth, in what is known as 'the Cambrian explosion'. The amount of time that it took these mountains to form is the same quantity of time that it took all life forms to evolve beyond the simple Pre Cambrian single cellular organisms. There's a lot of time looking at you in this pic!

Cambrian   Hill Farm, North Wales   March 08

One peculiarity of Britain's geology is that the further North and West one goes, the older the rock formations. At a positively *arriviste* 60-70 million years old, the Cretaceous and Quaternary rocks of the South East, created by millions of tiny creatures jam packed into sedimentary layers being trampled on by dinosaurs (!) gradually ascend to the heroic, dignified, isolate, ancient rock massifs of NW Scotland, W Wales and Cornwall.* Thus more or less mirroring the eventual retreat of Britain's first peoples out to the Celtic margins.

* Alas, when the Cambrian rocks were formed, Wales was actually adjacent to Newfoundland
and positioned somewhere near present day Namibia. Never mind!

Slate Quarry   Llanberis, N Wales   March 08

Cream Tea   Pass of Llanberis, N Wales   March 08

Llyn Gwynant   Snowdonia, N Wales   March 08

As If There Were No Tomorrow
The British Economy 2010

By a long way, the most important issue in Britain 2010 was the state of the economy. This article notes that economic cycles are a reality and that the correct management of an economy is a non-ideological matter. Many of the comments on the Labour government of the 2000s could apply equally to the United States Republican administration of the same period.

Datum (Fiscal Year / £ bn)

Year	GDP	Public Expenditure	National Debt
1997	830	318	348
2001	1,021	362	312
2007	1,398	544	500
2008	1,448	576	525
2010	1,474	661	772

'Do not blame the mirror for the ugly face you see in it'

In August 2009, Lord Adair Turner, Chairman of the Financial Services Authority (FSA) famously dubbed 'some of the City's activities' 'socially useless'. This raises the curious notion that the financial sector might somehow be socially useful?

The financial sector is not about social utility. It is about taking your money off you, using it to make their money and handing it back to you, less the cut that they have taken - gosh, what a shock! Be dumb enough to give the financiers the opportunity to exploit your greed and, of course, they will duly oblige, reflecting your greed back to you with interest. Caveat Emptor reigns.

But think that the economic crisis was conjured up by the City spivs, then, far away from their lunatic derivatives markets, look no further than the tripling of individual consumer credit during the 2000s. Think that it's only the City bonus culture at fault, siphoning £10bn pa out of the British economy, then in 2010 £9.9bn worth of personal bad debts were written off by banks and building societies. In 2008 City remunerations generated £68bn in taxes, 13.9% of total UK tax revenues from 3.7% of the workforce - no wonder the Treasury never challenged them. Think that the City is back to its usual rip off tricks, then think of the 130,000 jobs lost in the financial sector since 2008 and the £15bn hit delivered to the national tax take.

Think that the crisis was caused by socialist largesse, then look no further than the identical 3% Budget Deficits of George W's capitalist America. Seen the headline grabbing ' Public Sector's extra 1 million jobs', well not quite. In fact from 1997-2008, UK total employment increased from 26.5mn to 29.5mn jobs, within which Public Sector employment remained remarkably constant at 19%-20% of all jobs. The actual burgeoning of state employment over the period amounted to a much more modest 150,000 extra jobs.

Think that it was all due to Thatcherite right wing monetary liberalism then note that the American government sponsored mortgage suppliers, Fannie Mae & Freddie Mac, were commercialised in 1968 by a Democratic presidency and are now up to their necks in Alt A and subprime loans. And in 1999, Bill Clinton repealed the 1932 Glass Steagall Act which, in the wake of the Great Depression of 1929, had prohibited US financial institutions from combining investment banking, commercial banking and insurance.

Remember the ' More Tory than the Tories' left wing jibe at Tony Blair's 1997-2001 Labour Government? Indeed, it reduced National Debt to 30.5% of GDP and Public Expenditure to 34.7% of GDP, almost matching the 300 year National Debt low of 25.2% of GDP in 1991 and the post war Public Expenditure low of 34.2% of GDP of 1989, both attained at the end of the Thatcher years.

Think that it's due to householders being forced into raiding home equity by rip off Britain, then how come British householders were able to repay £24bn of mortgage debt in 2010 ? And how many householders over the last 30 years remonstrated against the social evil of astronomical house prices, whilst pocketing the proceeds?

Ever received a lawyer's, doctor's or dentist's bill in the last ten years? It's not only the financial sector that has propelled a more unequal Britain.

Think that the consumer society is at last going to get the Green message and consume less, then think of 1.2 billion materialistic, coal fuelled Chinese Comrades about to suffocate the global climate, and ramp commodity prices all over the planet.

'It's only when the tide goes out, you learn who's swimming naked' Warren Buffet 2001

All students of Economics are taught that the great lesson of the Great Depression of 1929 was that of Keynesian counter cyclical investment : that Governments should increase public expenditure to lift economies out of downturns, broadly the theory behind the various stimulus packages and bail outs since 2008. Doubtless the causes of the 2008 crash will be debated until the crack of doom, but the great lesson of the 2008 crash must surely be the reverse side of the Keynesian cycle - that the absolute, first priority in boom years must be to repay the debts incurred in crisis years.

Secondly, one has to critically reassess the signal given to European economies by the 1992 Maastricht Treaty : that Public Sector Budget Deficits should not exceed 3% of GDP and that National Debts should not exceed 60% of GDP.

Setting a limit for Public Sector Budget Deficits of 3% gives the implicit signal that a 3% Deficit is OK. Actually, and as many countries have now been finding out, a 3% Deficit is not OK - if a country runs a 3% Budget Deficit for 20 years, their National Debt would increase by 80%, (the origin of the Greek crisis).

The upper limit of National Debt at 60% of GDP is another wrong signal. Over a long history of global financial crises, rescue packages increase a National Debt by an average of 30%-50%

of GDP, more or less what is now happening to the British economy. Therefore, to avoid breaching the 60% limit in crisis conditions, the pre-crisis level of National Debt needs to be much lower, at 10%-20% of GDP. This is important because if National Debt lands in the 80% of GDP territory, it becomes chronic. Interest payments become a huge annual burden and the country gets stuck at permanently high debt levels.

Consequently, the economic guidelines for the European Community, laid down in the Maastricht treaty of 1992, are fundamentally flawed.

Thirdly, in the specific case of the British economy, the huge amounts of Home Equity Withdrawals in the 2000s had a major impact. From 2001-2007, and equivalent to 3.5% of GDP, the British householder sucked £300bn of wealth from the increased value of their houses. In addition, the British consumer added another £100bn of consumer credit over the period. Combining the two, and dwarfing City bonuses, the British consumer's annual stimulus package for the British economy amounted to 4.75% of GDP. On top of that, the Labour Government's spending spree of 2001-2008 increased the National Debt by £213 bn.

All up these three debt factors amounted to a £610bn economic stimulus, equivalent to 7.25% of GDP from 2001-2007. That is, the much vaunted economic miracle of the British economy never existed. There was no real growth of the British economy in the 2000s. It was a complete delusion.

In the 2000s, the British Government and the British people lived beyond its means.

Labour Budget Day   Treasury, Whitehall, London   March 24

'There's only three people here who have ever been through a recession'

Nicholas Macpherson (Head of Treasury Civil Service) to Alastair Darling upon becoming Chancellor of the Exchequer in 2007.

Who is responsible for the management of the economy ? The Hedge Funds ? The City spivs ? The 'too big to fail' banks ? Is it really the financial sector's job to run the economy ? No. There is only one entity responsible for the management of the economy and that, of course, is the Government. And the specific department of government instructed to manage the economy is the building you are looking at right now.

Did the Treasury know what was going on in the economy in the 2000s? Of course, they did. The Bank of England produces quarterly figures for Home Equity Withdrawals and consumer credit, the Treasury produces tax revenue and expenditure statistics monthly, and anyone could see what was happening to house prices. What on earth did the Treasury think was going on?

Nor should anyone be deceived by the new kid on the Whitehall block, the much trailed Office For Budget Responsibility - as if Budgetary Responsibility never existed beforehand . The Government and The Treasury have always had that responsibility - that is their job.

Gordon Brown, Chancellor of the Exchequer 1997-2007 and subsequently elected unopposed as Prime Minister by the Parliamentary Labour Party, made two great calls for the British economy - creating an independent Bank of England and keeping Britain out of the Euro, (Tony Blair would have taken Britain in). However in the 'Great Offices of State' series (BBC 2010), the reign of Gordon Brown at the Treasury was clinically dismantled.

Between the ministrations of an overbearing Chancellor, purging the old guard, and instituting an open plan office culture, the picture was painted of an organisation where social consensus and the massaging of political values became more important than the pure and direct contemplation of economic truth - the implicit allegation of the programme being that the Treasury completely lost its intellectual integrity under the Brown Chancellorship.

In the same vein, by September 2010, the nature of Lord Turner's comments had changed from the 'socially useless' financial sector to: ' Ill designed policy had been a much more powerful force than individual greed or error..... bonuses contributed to the financial crisis but were not its main cause...... we need to move beyond the demonisation of overpaid traders'

The case against the Government in the 2000s is not that of public expenditure splurge. Given the historically low level of National Debt at 30.5% of GDP in 2001, prima facie, a modest but focused expansion of national debt might not have seemed unreasonable to achieve long cherished social objectives. The real problem was the complete misreading of the economic situation. This meant that when the crisis eventually came the Ship of State slammed into the iceberg of economic reality, full steam ahead (overheated economy) and fully laden (locked in 3% budget deficit & massive consumer debt).

Obviously, the policy of public sector expansion in the 2000s had simply not countenanced what might happen in the event of a severe economic downturn - the most basic scenario for all economic planning from individual to household to world economy. And then, on top of that, all the signs of the impending crash were ignored.

The Treasury and the Government fell victim to that most fundamental of human errors : believing in their own propaganda, believing in the 'Thousand Year Reich' of British economic growth, the arrogant belief that their economic management skills had vanquished the economic cycle. This deluded viewpoint permeated

economic decisions at all levels throughout the 2000s and led the country to economic disaster. Therefore, the term 'socially useless' would more accurately apply to the Treasury and the Government's management of the economy, their record viciously condemned not by political diatribe, but by the actual economic facts.

If 'The Poll Tax' is on Margaret Thatcher's political tombstone, if 'The Iraq War' is on Tony Blair's, then Gordon Brown's political epitaph would surely read 'No More Boom And Bust'

Yesterday vs Tomorrow
The British Economy   Budget Day, March 2010

'People know there is a deficit, they know it needs to come down and if you deny that, frankly, people will not listen to you. They will walk away and it will have disastrous consequences next time you go to the polls'
Alastair Darling to the post 2010 election Labour Party Conference.

Karl Marx, quite correctly, addressed the eternal conflict between Capital and Labour, but he could not have foreseen the emergence of modern 'State Capitalism', with States of all types collecting huge tax takes, commanding massive budgets, accumulating vast amounts of capital, and employing millions of people. 'State Capitalism' is more obvious in a centralised command economy like Communist China, where business is in the service of State power and where workers are typically exploited by a wealthy and unaccountable elite. But it is unusual to think of our own governments in this way. In 2010, the FTSE 350 (the top 350 companies) was capitalised at c.£2,000bn. At a total asset value of c.£1,000bn, UK Gov / 'UK State Capitalism' is about the same size as the top 17 companies in the FTSE 100, equivalent to 17 huge, nasty, multinational globalised capitalist beasts spreading their rapacious tentacles all over the planet?

With such asset values to protect and such running costs to control, it is inevitable that 'State Capitalism' will be pitched against the interests of labour and Britain is at the start of a long 20-30 year battle between the taxpayer and the public sector worker, between 'the people' and 'the workers'. It will cut across Governments of all political complexions and it will not go away .

£43,000,000,000.00 / Forty three billion pounds -
In 2010, 3p in every £1 earned by a British worker went to pay interest payments on the National Debt. This could have paid for:

5 Iraq Wars at £8bn per war, or...
172 Super Hospitals at £250mn, or... etc...
1,720 brand new schools at £25mn
£83 per week for 10 million pensioners
285,000 social housing units at £150,000
1,228,000 nurses at £35,000 pa
60 off 75 turbine wind farms at £725mn
80% of the motorway network completely rebuilt at £25mn per mile

In 2011 the interest payments will rocket to a very frightening £71bn.

Labour Budget Day   House of Commons, Westminster, London   March 24

In other words, contrary to publicly received 'socialist auto non-think', Public Sector cuts at times of excessive National Debt are in fact Pro-Socialist. They minimise the waste of taxpayer's precious resources and conserve the national asset platform for future social expenditure. Paradoxically, liberal/progressives should be at the forefront of demanding National Debt reduction, as the best way to build the schools, health service and welfare state of the future.

In fact, given that Public Sector workers will be pensioners themselves in decades to come, it is even in their own self interest to straighten out the public finances in the short term, so that they can benefit in the long term.

As for employment in the Public Sector, contrary to received opinion, Civil Service numbers only increased 3% from 1997-2008, well below the 11.3% rise in total UK employment. Public Sector vs Private Sector wages is a tricky area, but the ONS's own figures for 2010 state that Public Sector average wages were £554 per week, as against Private Sector's £473 per week - from lagging 5% behind in 2002 to forging 17% ahead in 2010. On top of that the proportion of GDP devoted to public sector pensions increased

from 5.9% to 6.9%, in cash terms, a transfer of resources in their favour of £14bn pa.

There is further anecdotal evidence that the public sector was buttered up during the Labour era. In 2010, 9,000 public sector employees earned more than the Prime Minister's £142,500 pa; 38,000 employees earned more than £100,000 pa and 1,000 employees earned more than £200,000 pa. Famously, a South London primary school head teacher earned £200,000 in one year.

Broadly speaking, without wrangling over every point, one can safely say that the public sector worker did not do too badly under Labour.

In the short term, the overriding national economic objective has to be to ensure that the National Debt does not become chronic and impose a 3%-5% tax on all taxpayers for the next 30-40 years. The policies of the Conservative / Lib Dem Coalition, on the very debatable assumption that they all go to plan, will leave the National Debt in 2014-2015 hovering dangerously around the chronic threshold of 60%-70% of GDP. Many would argue that

that is totally unfair on future generations and that much tougher policies are mandatory.

Add the impending economic burden of a rapidly ageing population, add the looming spectre of structural unemployment, and against the objective requirements of such massive facts, the current Labour Party and Trade Union stance, carping about any further cuts than in their March 2010 budget comes across as self-contradictory and economically delusional. - unless of course one believes in an even more massive National Debt or unless one believes in an even higher national standard of living than the one that Britain has already not earned.

Up to a point, one can sympathise with Labour's predicament - admitting that they got the economy wrong would be tantamount to admitting that their expenditure programme on Health, Education and Public Services was likewise wrong. One should not expect an admission that legitimately held core values are 'wrong'.

However it should not be forgotten that the high interest rate / strong pound policy of the 1997-2001 Labour Administration, decimated the manufacturing sector and ramped the services sector. Financial services, much feted by the Labour government, were at the forefront of their modernisation policy for the British economy. Labour presided over the enshrinement of the almighty financial services sector during the 2000s, in charge of an economy and of policies that funnelled huge amounts of private and public funds into the financier's vaults. Therefore every time the Labour Party subsequently pointed the finger of blame for the 2008 crisis at the financial sector, one could only wince in intellectual agony.

As the incumbent government during the crisis and for the ten years leading up to it, they have a duty to the country to set the record straight. The specific failure that they have to own up to is that they busted the Keynesian bargain - that Government cannot overspend in the recession <u>and also</u> overspend in the boom. It is very important that the Labour Party acknowledges that this limit to Public Expenditure exists and that that limit was breached on their watch. It is in the national interest that Labour go on the record with this admission. It needs to be hard wired into the future economic policy of the country, whichever political party is in power.

Now in Opposition, it is Labour's duty to oppose and present alternative policies, but this does not justify a Pavlovian opposition to everything. Therefore, what would really impress the world would be to see Labour putting their weight to the wheel of national reconstruction, being big enough to admit that the problem is bigger than any party differences, and ensuring that the hugely important job of National Debt reduction gets done for the future of the country.

'Those whom the Gods wish to destroy, they first of all turn mad' Ancient

Goldman Sachs, quite correctly, values its commercial property portfolio at 50% of current market value, because that's how far property prices can fall in a severe economic downturn, as occurred in the Japanese bubble economy crash of the early 1990s. Only relatively recently, in the UK 'negative equity' property crash of the early 1990s, 1.8 million British householders experienced plummeting house values of up to 20%.

Up to a point, householders who needed to move house in 2006-07 fell victim to negative equity because of the overblown state of the housing market. However, one suspects that far more were 'on the make' in that market, cashing in on the bonanza value of their properties or upscaling to grander spreads, ignoring the risks they were taking. A householder bonus culture would not be an inaccurate description.

Evidently not content with merely being overextended at the top of the market, householders then took out Home Equity Withdrawal policies en masse. Only total amnesia of the recent past, or total denial of the possibility of a property crash could explain why those householders failed to ask the IQ Level 3 question : ' What happens if house prices go down ?' Not only negative equity against the mortgage, but also a huge loan from the bank on top. Intelligence is not the first word that comes to mind. It's very hard to have any sympathy for such stupidity.

In addition, from 1997-2008, whilst inflation only increased by 35%, consumer credit, mainly on credit cards, tripled from £85bn to £233bn. Similarly with total national personal debt, tripling from £500bn to £1,457bn.

Not surprisingly, Personal Insolvencies have now hit record levels : 135,000 in 2010 - 110,000 for debts of over £15,000 and 25,000 Debt Relief Orders for debts under £15,000. All of this feeding into the bank and building society write downs of £9.9bn in 2010, which the rest of society ultimately has to stump up for.

Obviously, the post crash years have been a sobering experience for many consumers and households. Perhaps sober is the keyword that might explain how the otherwise restrained, common sense British public took complete leave of its senses.

Pumped up, jumped up, junked up, hung up, drugged up, boozed up, strung out in social network fantasy land, dancing the mesmeric beat of the sense culture, dumping the solid, the real, the everyday - the lonely millions at the mercy of every last dream peddler jerk of consumerism, the ultimate apotheosis, the consumer society consumed.

'We all knew about it. We all worried about it. No one did anything about it' Jamie Dimon, Chairman & CEO, JP Morgan

The argument in this article is incomplete without a clear idea of what would have happened to the British economy if it had been correctly managed in the years running up to the crisis during the 2000s.

Let us assume that the economic cycle delivered the 2008 crisis in exactly the way it did - the run on Northern rock in September 2007, the collapse of Lehman Brothers in September 2008, the bail out of RBS and Lloyds-HBOS in October 2008 etc.

But let us assume that consumers, banks, businesses, workers, civil servants and government had previously applied the other half of the Keynesian bargain - paying off their debts in the boom years - what then would have happened?

- The rational British Consumer would not have put that extra £100bn debt onto their credit cards, at say £20bn pa, effectively deflating the 2000s economy by 1.5% pa.

- At the minimum for guaranteeing legitimate business propositions and releasing liquidity for the elderly, the rational British

householder would have taken out £25bn pa less in Home Equity. Withdrawals, deflating the 2000s economy by a further 2% pa.

- Thus deflated by 3.5% pa, the economy would have been barely growing. Now in the real world, the Government's public expenditure options would have been drastically curtailed and it could never have justified a substantial increase in the National Debt. Besides, had the Maastricht conditions been much tougher, as they need to be, then the Government expenditure programme would never have withstood a National Debt stress test.

- Obviously, house price rises would have moderated in less pumped up economic conditions. And if that hadn't restored sanity to the property market, then the government's solemn duty would have been to crush the property boom. Why ? Because of what subsequently happened to the British householder by failing to do just that.

So, if the Government had entered the 2007/2008 crisis with a Budget surplus, a declining National Debt and with consumers and businesses with manageable levels of debt and cash savings for a rainy day, how then would the post crash crisis have played out ?

Firstly, consumers would have carried on consuming without the huge panic cut backs on household budgets that have tanked the post crash economy. This in turn would have delivered a steadier economy and a reliable basis for planning the recovery. Britain might not have avoided a serious recession, but it would have not have been the disaster that we now have on our hands. Consumers would have played a huge part in a much more speedy recovery, simply by continuing to consume and thereby maintaining tax revenues.

Secondly, with a Budget Surplus upon entering the crisis, the Government could now have legitimately justified a Budget Deficit, secure in the knowledge that that deficit would be used for its only legitimate purpose - stimulating an economy in crisis. More importantly, rather then being forced to reduce staff, the Government would now be increasing public sector employment as part of the counter-cyclical boost to the economy. Top of the list, a surge in national house building, to crush property prices down to equilibrium, whereby first time buyers, rural locals and service staff can get into the housing market.

The pre-crash Government Budget Deficit and the UK consumer debt have been the killers for the British post-crash economy. This in turn was caused by the complete misreading of the 2000s economic situation, which in turn was caused by a lack of clarity about fundamental economic policy. This in turn was caused by the imposition of values and beliefs onto hard economic fact.

Values may be admirable but they are only projections onto the world. They are not actual Reality itself. Alas, Yesterday was a bubble of prosperity and, as a result, Tomorrow will be a very, very long Reality Check - whichever party is in power.

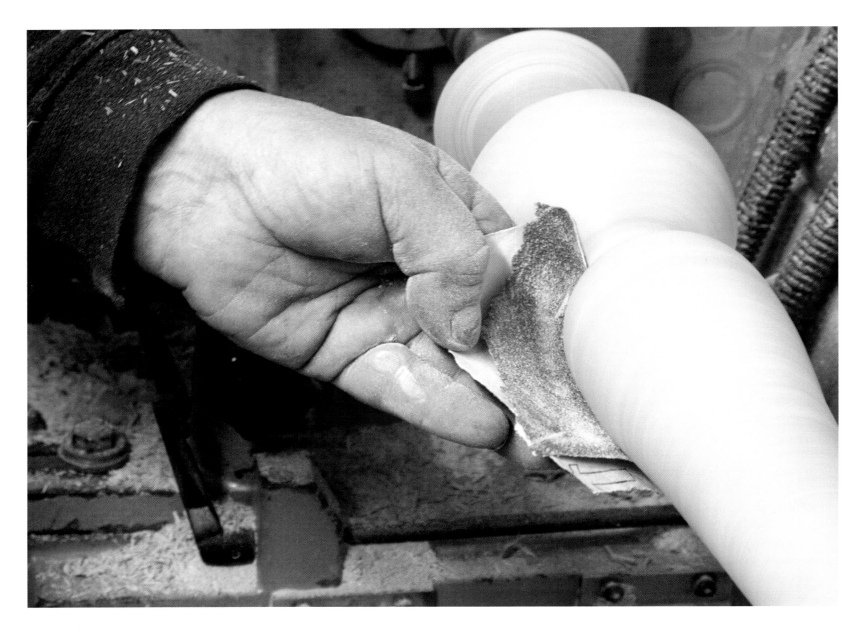

Sanding   Phillip Moss, Joiner   Dobson's, Oldham   March 25

Turning   Phillip Moss, Joiner   Dobson's, Oldham   March 25

Instrument   Darren Holt, Printer   Brown's CTP, Middleton   March 25

Chemical   Darren Holt, Printer   Brown's CTP, Middleton   March 25

Weight   Darren Holt, Printer   Brown's CTP, Middleton   March 25

Space   Marion Thomson, Abstract Artist   Sheffield   March 31

Texture   Marion Thomson, Abstract Artist   Sheffield   March 31

Shape   Marion Thomson, Abstract Artist   Sheffield   March 31

Never Alone   Anfield, Liverpool   March 28

Alone 'Another Place', Antony Gormley Crosby, Merseyside March 28

God Created St Mary's Whaplode, Lincolnshire April 30

april

St Augustine's Cross   Ebbsfleet, Thanet, Kent   Good Friday

Dispatched by Pope Gregory I on what might nowadays be called a revival mission, the cross commemorates the place where, in 597, St Augustine and his companions first held mass after landing in England. This is generally viewed as marking the rebirth of Christianity in Southern England, which had lapsed since the end of the Roman occupation of Britain c. 410.

Supported by Aethelbert, King of Kent, and Bertha, his Christian wife, St Augustine founded the abbey in Canterbury, became the first Archbishop of Canterbury and, vested in him by Pope Gregory, asserted authority over the other churches in Britain to varying effect.

Cloisters   Canterbury Cathedral   Good Friday

And He found in the temple those who were selling oxen and sheep and doves... He poured out the coins of the money changers and overturned their tables... And to those who were selling the doves He said, "Take these things away; stop making My Father's house a place of business." John 2:14-17

Oxen and Sheep and Doves   Canterbury Cathedral   Good Friday

Awe York Minster Good Friday

Chorister York Minster Good Friday

The Cross					York Minster					Good Friday

Loch Lomond   Scotland   April 03

Loch Scridain   Isle of Mull, Scotland   Easter Sunday

Go Tell It On The Mountain   Isle of Iona   Easter Sunday

The Power Of Place   Iona Abbey, Isle of Iona, Scotland   Easter Sunday

In 563, exiling himself from tragic events in Ireland and making the sea crossing in a wicker coracle covered in leather, St Columba came to Iona with twelve companions, and founded the original Iona monastery, which served as a major centre for the spread of Christianity among the Picts and Scots.. The Book of Kells, the famous illuminated manuscript is believed to have been produced by the monks of Iona in the years leading up to 800.   The Chroncile of Ireland was also produced at Iona until about 740.

In 806, Vikings massacred 68 monks in Martyrs' Bay, and Columba's monks returned to Ireland, to the Monastery at Kells and to monasteries in Belgium, France, and Switzerland.

In 825, St Blaithmac and those monks who had returned with him to Iona, were martyred by a further Viking raid. The Abbey was burned down and Iona became deserted.

Reconsecrated from 1200 onwards, and then abandoned in the Scottish Reformation of the 1500's, the present day abbey of Iona dates from the 1930s and the setting up of the Iona community as an ecumenical Christian community.

Kings were crowned on Iona and many early Scottish Kings and Chiefs, including Duncan the victim of Macbeth, were buried in the Abbey graveyard - with kings from Ireland, Norway and France, thought to number 48 kings in all.

And Jesus got up, rebuked the wind and said to the waves, 'Quiet! Be still!'
Then the wind died down and it was completely calm. He said to his disciples,
'Why are you so afraid? Do you still have no faith?'   (Mark 4 : 39-40)

The Stilling   Isle of Iona   Easter Sunday

Be Still   Cloisters, Iona Abbey   Easter Sunday

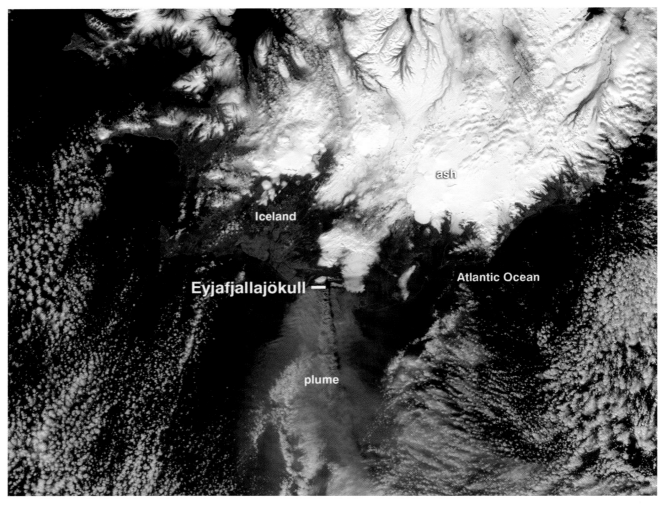

Volcano   Eyjafjallajökull, Iceland   April 15

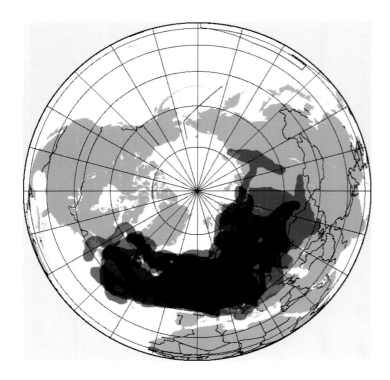

Due to a freakish set of circumstances, the volcanic ash cloud from the Icelandic volcano Eyjfjallajökull, caused the biggest shutdown of European airspace since World War II. Millions of passengers were stranded in Europe and across the world for days on end. It cost the airline industry c.£1.5bn in compensation and trading losses. (NASA pic)

Erupting beneath glacial ice, the lava not only reacted violently with the glacial melt water to explode the ash cloud miles into the air but the ice cold water also freeze dried the volcanic ash into trillions of silicon particles. These then fed into an unusually stable South East Jet Stream which ferried the ash cloud directly into some of the busiest airspace in the world.

If you want to see multi-coloured striped fields of tulips being readied for the British market, then go to Holland. 'You've arrived twenty five years too late' was the comment about the almost total disappearance of Spalding's tulip heritage.

From the 2,000 acres of tulips grown as recently as 1985, just a few acres now remain under cultivation, largely for the annual flower festival.

Moving with the times, David Bowman's of Spalding are now Europe's largest pumpkin producers, growing two million pumpkins annually for Britain and across Europe - the 50 year old Spalding Tulip Parade in May has now been matched by the Pumpkin Festival each October.

Not requiring a stone free soil for modern automated picking, daffodil and narcissi cultivation is still flourishing.

Spalding Tulips   Spalding, Lincolnshire   April 30

Earth   Lincolnshire   April 30

Based on the fertility of its land and quietly going about its business, Lincolnshire has always been
one of the wealthier parts of Britain. The Anglo Saxons were adept at spinning and weaving and there
is growing evidence of a substantial wool industry in Lincolnshire at that time. In the Middlle Ages,
sheep farming and the wool trade brought untold wealth to the county and churches of breathtaking
beauty were built.

Lincoln became England's sixth largest city as woolen goods were exported through the nearby port of
Boston. Lincoln was famous for its red fabrics - the wool was extremely fine and Lincoln Scarlett was
the most expensive material on the Italian market. Florentine merchants visited England frequently
and Lincolnshire was the source for over 50% of the wool exported there. Lincoln Green, a woolen
cloth dyed with woad and weld, was famously associated with Robin Hood and his Merry Men.

In the seventeenth century the Longwool sheep became significantly more important, and huge
amounts of longwool were transported to Norfolk, for the worsted trade there.

Originally set up to support the Crusades (1095 - 1272) and with a lethal combination of military prowess, religious zeal and financial acumen, the Western Christian Military Order of the Knights Templar grew to become, arguably, the first multinational corporation.

Officially endorsed by the Pope in 1129, the Order became a favoured charity for Christians, grew rapidly in membership and power, and established financial networks across the whole of Christendom. Not unlike letters of credit, the system that enabled Knights to deposit assets in one country and then cash them at the Templar headquarters in Jerusalem represented an early form of banking.

Whilst theTemplar knights, in their distinctive white mantles with a red cross, were among the most skilled fighting units of the Crusades, the Templar organisation itself acquired large tracts of land, both in Europe and the Middle East; bought and managed farms and vineyards; built churches and castles; were involved in manufacturing, import and export; had their own fleet of ships; and at one point they even owned the entire island of Cyprus.

At Temple Bruer, the Templars were leaders in the sheep farming industry, an economic powerhouse that made Lincolnshire a rich county at a time when Lincolnshire was populous and, economically, a leading part of England.

That economic growth broadly coincided with the end of the Crusades, the reason for the Templars' existence. However the Templars' wealth remained and whilst they moved into banking, some potentates were reluctant to repay monies borrowed and a general jealousy of the Templars' wealth developed.

Not exactly the Goldman Sachs of their day, nevertheless the Templars suffered the distinctive fate reserved for all over-mighty bankers. In January 1308, Edward II sent knights to arrest the monk-knights for alleged crimes, none of which were substantiated. The community at Temple Bruer was broken up and their assets seized. And in France, with a huge national debt owing large amounts directly to the Templars, King Philip IV defaulted on his debts by pressurizing Pope Clement V to disband the Templars, and then burnt their leaders at the stake.

Knights Templar · · · · · · · Temple Bruer, Lincolnshire · · · · · · · April 30

Transcept
Lincoln Cathedral
April 30

24. It is easier for a camel to go through the eye of a needle than for a
rich man to enter the Kingdom of Heaven.   Matthew 19:24

Through The Eye Of A Needle   Lincoln Cathedral   April 30

Etheldreda, Abbess of Ely   Ely Cathedral, Cambridgeshire   April 30

Altar Screen   Ely Cathedral, Cambridgeshire   April 30

Born at Exning in Suffolk c.636 AD, and brought up in an atmosphere of piety as the daughter of Saewara and the Christian King Anna of East Anglia, Etheldreda's sole ambition was to become a nun, but she was destined not to attain this goal until twice married. Firstly, on the basis of respect for her monastic vocation and upon the transference of the estate of Ely to her name, to King Tondbert of South Gyrwe, a subkingdom in the Fens. And secondly to Egfrith, the child Prince and eventual King of Northumbria.

Egfrith adored Ethedreda but his respect for her saintliness and celibate way of life could not restrain the desires of manhood ; Egfrith persisted with the inevitable result. Etheldreda took flight on a long and legendary journey southwards and, after many days of weary walking, the saint arrived on her own lands on the Isle of Ely. Here, there was a piece of good, firm, rich land, supporting six hundred families and surrounded to a great distance by fens, a more formidable rampart than walls or plain water.

In AD 673, Etheldreda built a large double monastery and, with special Papal privilege and the support of her great friend, St Wilfred, ruled over the monastery for seven years, setting a great example of piety, abstinence and spiritual guidance until passing away in June 679.

Her successors were princesses of the same family and the abbey of Ely was, for many years, very famous and very rich. It was constituted as a cathedral in 1109, the abbot and bishop thenceforth becoming one person.

Ely Cathedral   Ely Cathedral, Cambridgeshire   April 30

Octagon   Ely Cathedral, Cambridgeshire   April 30

Perpendicular   Ely Cathedral, Cambridgeshire   April 30

Town Centre   Stourbridge, W Midlands   May 06

may

THE PHILOSOPHERS HAVE ONLY INTERPRETED THE WORLD IN VARIOUS WAYS · THE POINT HOWEVER IS TO CHANGE IT ·

Karl Marx   Labour Day, Highgate Cemetery, London   May 01

Karl Marx   Labour Day, Highgate Cemetery, London   May 01

To its great credit, British culture has always had the capacity to nurture the most diverse points of view, in this instance the historic socialist argument.   There has always been a strong radical and left wing contribution to the British political debate, and Karl Marx's ideas were able to flourish within this climate. Broadly speaking, there can be little doubt that this body of ideas had a huge impact on societies in the twentieth century.

Alas and alack, it is the fate of all great ideas to depend on mere human beings for their implementation, and the concentration of power in the apparatus of the various Communist States that arose, invariably presented the earthlings involved with the irresistible temptations of power and patronage.   Forty years of putting up with this in Soviet Eastern Europe was cynically summed up as follows :

" Capitalism is exploitation of Man by Man !!!!

   Communism is .... other way round . "

By Trimpley Village Hall Polling Station 7:00 am   Wyre Forest   May 06

The Battle Of Middle England   -   General Election, May 06, 2010

Edgbaston - Labour   Stourbridge - Labour
Solihull - Lib/Dem   Wyre Forest - Independent

Conservative / UKIP   Stourbridge   May 06

        Labour   Stourbridge   May 06

Early Morning Rush   Wyre Forest   May 06

In 1998, Worcestershire health authority proposed closing Accident & Emeregency and all acute inpatient services at Kidderminster General Hospital, where Dr Richard Taylor used to work as a Consultant. This meant that all seriously ill local patients would have to travel many miles to hospitals in Worcester, Redditch, or Dudley :

" This was simply a complete and utter disregard for the people and I felt that something must be done about it. "

Campaigning on a single issue, to save the local Kidderminster Hospital, Dr Taylor was elected in 2001 to represent Wyre Forest with a landslide majority of 18,000, which ousted a Junior Government Minister, and, in the subsequent election in 2005, Dr Taylor became the only Independent MP since 1949 to have retained his seat for a second term.

"I used to be totally uninterested in politics, My career move into politics was fired by complete and utter anger that a very few ill informed people had the right to take away a vital service for a population of 140,000 and wrap it up in spin."

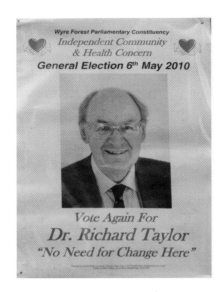

The Hospital That Dr Richard Taylor Saved   Wyre Forest   May 06

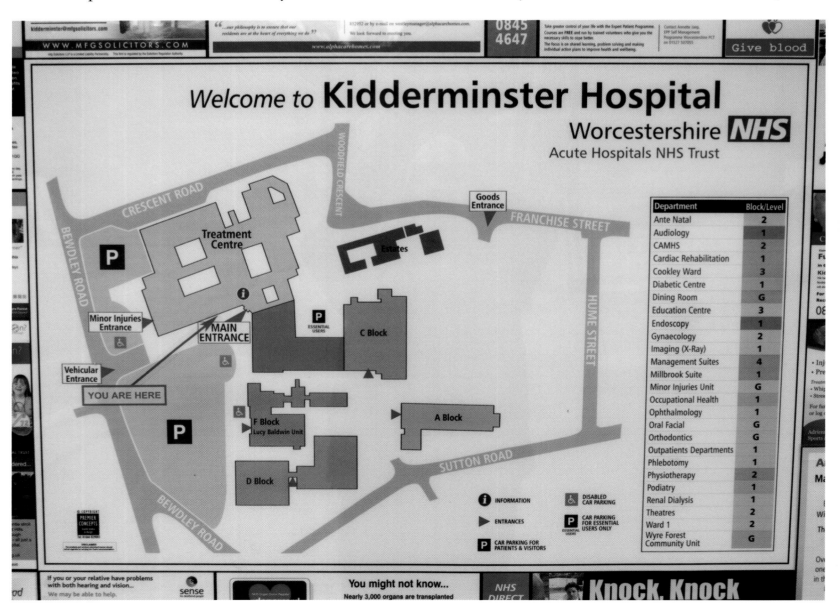

Lib Dems   Solihull   May 06

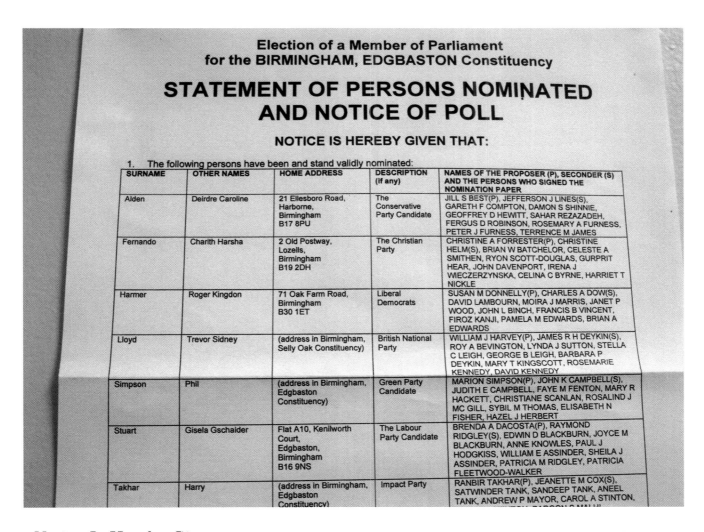

Notice Is Hereby Given   Edgbaston   May 06

Walking The Dogs   Wyre Forest   May 06

High Rise   Edgbaston   May 06

Family Outing   Solihull   May 06

Students   Edgbaston   May 06

Evening Queues   Solihull   May 06

As long queues formed in the evening, an acute problem arose at a small number of polling stations, and at 10pm doors to some polling stations were closed with understandably angry voters locked out and deprived of voting.

1,200 voters at 27 polling stations in 16 constituencies were affected and a major investigation was carried out by the Electoral Commission.

Although one suspects that modern 'late nite' twenty four hour Britain was at least partially to blame, the Commission concluded that the problem was mainly caused by maladministration at the local electoral level and various practical measures have been proposed. Chief among these that the law should be changed to allow people still queuing at polling stations at 10pm to be able to vote.

Polling Station In Bloom   Solihull   May 06

Ballot Boxes   Wyre Forest   May 06

The Vote   Wyre Forest   May 06

The Returning Officer   Wyre Forest   May 06

The Count   Wyre Forest   May 06

| Scrutineering | Wyre Forest | May 06 |

As the polls closed at 10pm, the BBC 10 o'clock news announced yet another stunningly
accurate forecast by the joint BBC/ITV Exit Poll * :

	Exit Poll	Actual Result
Conservatives	307	307
Labour	255	258
Lib/Dems	59	57
Others	29	28

This confirmed all the predictions that a 'hung parliament' in the House of Commons
would result without any party commanding an absolute majority and that the
Conservatives would not be immediately forming the next government.

It also brutally dashed the hopes of a Lib/Dem breakthrough, expectations of which
had oscillated wildly during the election campaign.

* In the 2005 General Election, BBC and ITV agreed for the first time to pool their
respective data, using results from Mori and NOP. The Exit Poll method involved more
than twenty thousand people being interviewed at one hundred and twenty polling stations
across the country It predicted the 66 seat Labour majority with 100% accuracy.

Although the Conservatives (below) were justifiably confident in expecting to gain the Wyre Forest constituency, nevertheless the mixed fortunes of a complex Election night unfolded in these four West Midlands constituencies.

Dr Richard Taylor's valiant stand in Wyre Forest was brought to an end as the Conservative tide swept away his tenure with a 2,643 vote majority for Mark Garnier, successful at his second attempt.

Margot James, an excellently qualified local person and not disadvantaged by her prominent position in Britain's top 100 gay list, easily gained Stourbridge for the Conservatives from Labour's Lynda Waltho, whose 407 vote majority of 2005 was trounced by a Conservative majority of 5,164.

However, one of Labour's best defences of the night occurred in Birmingham, Edgbaston, where Gisela Stuart confounded the 5% national swing to the Conservatives with an adverse swing of only 1.3%, and a reduced but defensible majority of 1,274 votes. The Labour heartland stayed staunch and it was results like this that prevented annihilation for Labour, delivering them a credible platform for winning the next general election with an absolute majority.

Similarly, one of the Lib/Dems best results for the night (and conversely one of the worst results for the Conservatives) was for Lorelei Burt to hold on to Solihull with her perilous 279 vote majority, now hanging even more perilously by 175 votes. Both the Lib/Dems and Conservatives in Solihull gained an extra 3,000 votes, equally from Labour and from a high voter turnout.

Sensing Victory

Wyre Forest

May 06

I Hereby Declare   Wyre Forest   May 06

Ian Miller, the Returning Officer for the Wyre Forest Constituency,
declares the result of the vote:

Conservative	Mark Garnier	18,793 votes
Health Concern	Richard Taylor	16,115
Labour	Nigel Knowles	7,298
Lib/Dems	Neville Farmer	6,040
UKIP	Michael Wrench	1,498
BNP	Gordon Howells	1,120

In the traditional display of humility, Mark Garnier MP vows to serve the people of Wyre Forest, expresses great appreciation for the work of the outgoing MP, and praises the efforts of the Returning Officer and his team.

On his way up to the stage, Dr Richard Taylor (centre) muttered about having to find a new career. Gordon Howells of the BNP (left of Dr Taylor) looks on.

Proportional Representation : although voting patterns would have been substantially different had it been in operation, a purely theoretical PR interpretation of the 2010 General Election vote would have been :

	Votes	MPs
Conservatives	10,710,000	234
Labour	8,600,000	188
Lib/Dems	6,830,000	149
UKIP	918,000	20
BNP	568,000	12
SNP	491.000	11
Green	285,000	6

(Total Vote : 29,700,000 = 45,800 for each of 650 seats)

In the above, the number of Conservative MPs would have been cut down by 73, but had the same logic been applied to the 2005 Election, Labour's absolute majority of 355 MPs would have been slashed even further by 126 MPs, down to a coalition forming 229 seats.

The liberally inclined should also note that the extreme right British National Party (BNP) would have had twice as many MPs as the Green party.

I Would Like To Thank   Wyre Forest   May 06

Has Anything Actually Happened?   Jon Sopel, BBC News Presenter

Did Something Happen?   Media and Public Scrum

After five days of continuous 24 hour news coverage about virtually nothing...

Endless Interview No: 3571   Wired To The World

Somehow Still Immaculate   Mishal Hussein, BBC News Presenter

On the sixth day, The Demos said : 'Let there be ...

DAILY EXPRESS

THE WORLD'S GREATEST NEWSPAPER · express.co.uk · WEATHER: SUNSHINE AND SHOWERS · THURSDAY MAY 13, 2010 40p

Snow falls in coldest May for 17 years
SEE PAGE 23

Scandal of the TV lessons in how to sponge off Britain
SEE PAGE 15

IT'S LOVE

Now let's hope Dave and Nick's brave new world is a winner

David Cameron and his deputy Nick Clegg smiling on the first day of their historic coalition government in Downing Street yesterday

By Macer Hall Political Editor

SMILING side by side yesterday, David Cameron and Nick Clegg ushered in an extraordinary era of "new politics" at Westminster.

The Tory Prime Minister and his Lib Dem deputy shook hands in a display of personal chemistry that sealed the birth of Britain's first coalition government since the days of Winston Churchill.

Mr Cameron described their deal as a "historic and seismic shift" in the British political landscape. And he

got to work appointing a new Cabinet with five senior Liberal Democrats in top jobs.

A pledge to slash Britain's record deficit is at the heart of the Government's plan of action.

Chancellor George Osborne moved in at the Treasury with Lib Dem David Laws as his number two in the role of Chief Secretary to the Treasury while Vince Cable was handed the Business Secretary portfolio. In a surprise

TURN TO PAGE 2

Noemie Lenoir, 30, was found unconscious

M&S beauty in suicide bid
SEE PAGE 11

THE Sun

Thursday, May 13, 2010 · 25p · thesun.co.uk

David Cameron THE JOURNEY
AN INTIMATE 12-PAGE PORTRAIT IN PICTURES

Cheryl's brother held on gun raid
SEE PAGE 11

EUROPA LEAGUE FINAL
A MADRID...2
FULHAM......1
AFTER EXTRA TIME

NO JOY FOR ROY'S BOYS

THEY'RE THE BIGGEST DOUBLE ACT SINCE MORECAMBE AND WISE. NOW CAMERON AND CLEGG HAD BETTER BLOODY WELL...

BRING US SUNSHINE

By TOM NEWTON DUNN Political Editor

DAVID Cameron and Nick Clegg vowed to bring us a brighter Britain yesterday as the nation's biggest double act got down to work.

As well as facing up to the serious problems threatening our country, the PM and his deputy used humour and togetherness to usher in what they called "a new politics".

They also pledged "co-operation over confrontation" as they launched the historic Tory-Lib Dem coalition in Downing Street.

SEE PAGES 4, 5, 6, 7, 8 & 9

Partners . . pair at No 10 yesterday

Cameron's first day **20 pages** of news & analysis

The Daily Telegraph

Thursday, May 13, 2010 · NEWSPAPER OF THE YEAR · No.48,193 £1.00

A special relationship

Cameron at No10

- Cameron and Clegg forge a close bond at coalition launch
- Lib Dems are given five senior posts in new administration
- Theresa May, Home Secretary, and a job for Duncan Smith

By Andrew Porter Political Editor

A laughing matter: Mr Cameron is embarrassed at a press conference in the Downing Street garden yesterday after being reminded that once when asked for his favourite political joke he had replied "Nick Clegg"

Men of different cloths, sharing the pulpit

Andrew Gimson Sketch

DOUBLE MEASURE

TWO BESPOKE SUITS

TWO BESPOKE SHIRTS

TWO BESPOKE TIES

£995

SARTORIANI

EXCLUSIVE Brown answered the phone and we could hear him saying 'Nick, Nick, I can't hold on any longer. Nick, I've got to go to the palace'.

Martin Argles's remarkable fly-on-the-wall photo essay on Brown's last hours in No 10. Pages 21-24

£1.00
Thursday 13.05.10
Published in London and Manchester
guardian.co.uk

theguardian

So, Prime Minister, what's changed since you described your new political soulmate as a joke?

Meeting the press in the garden of No 10, David Cameron was reminded that when asked for his favourite political joke, he once replied: 'Nick Clegg'. His deputy pretended to storm off *Photograph: Charles Bibby*

The happy couple at No 10

- Leaders unveil plan focused on reducing deficit
- Clegg oversees agenda to bring in political reform

Patrick Wintour Political editor

Nick Clegg is to take personal charge of a massive programme of constitutional renewal, including a referendum bill on electoral reform passed by summer 2011, in what the prime minister, David Cameron, described yesterday as a Liberal-Conservative government that marks a "historic and seismic shift" in British politics.

On yet another breathless day at Westminster, Cameron and his deputy prime minister Clegg held a joint press conference in which both displayed equal enthusiasm for turning their short-

gun marriage brought about by a hung parliament, into a genuine partnership.

Cameron said the government would end the chronic short-termism in British politics.

Clegg said: "Until today we were rivals, and now we are colleagues. And that says a lot about the new politics which is now beginning to unfold. This is a new government and a new kind of government."

...and already we've had the first domestic

Jill Treanor and Larry Elliott
Full story, page 5 **|** Viewpoint, page 33 ▶

2-17 ▶▶

Continued on page 2 ▶

DAILY Mirror — Thursday May 13, 2010 — REAL NEWS. REAL ENTERTAINMENT — 45p

M&S girl ODs on pills and booze

SEE PAGE 3

ODD COUPLE
Cameron and Clegg meet at No 10 yesterday

HIS TORY BOYS

..but how long will the love-in last?

By BOB ROBERTS, Political Editor

DAVID Cameron and No2 Nick Clegg pose at No10 yesterday – as they boast their double act will lead Britain in a "historic new direction".

Their love-in saw them stage a jokey show to swap jokes at a press conference. However, there were sign of uneasiness in the truce as the Tory leader offered to "swallow humble pie" for ridiculing Mr Clegg as "a joke" before the election.

The Deputy PM is one of five Lib Dem ministers in the new Cabinet. In return his party will back £6billion Tory cuts that could cost hundreds of thousands of jobs and see savage reductions in child tax credit. Mr Cameron claimed the new government would be "strong and stable". Mr Clegg added: "We will show the sceptics we predict it will go wrong that they are wrong."

But former Tory chairman Lord Tebbit warned bleakly: "It will not last many years. As they say - marry in haste and repent at leisure."

FULL STORY INSIDE

Daily Mail — THURSDAY, MAY 13, 2010 — www.dailymail.co.uk — 50p

£1M MUST BE WON

WIN £50,000

GUARANTEED EVERY DAY!

MEET OUR LATEST WINNER ON PAGE 41

Laughing and joking at an extraordinary Downing St press call best buddies Dave and Nick present ...the Liberal Conservatives

THE GREAT NO.10 LOVE-IN

Whoops: David Cameron's face says it all as his description of Nick Clegg as a 'political joke' comes back to haunt him yesterday

By James Chapman
Political Editor

SIDE by side they stood in the sun-dappled Downing Street garden.

It was their first public appearance as the couple in charge of the first British coalition Government since the war.

Sharing jokes, exchanging meaningful glances and referring to each other chummily as Nick and David, they couldn't have looked happier.

This was Day One of what Prime Minister David Cameron now describes as 'the Liberal-Conservative Government'. There was one sticky moment, when Mr Cameron was reminded by a tactless journalist that he had once described his new coalition partner as 'my favourite political joke'.

But such was the mood of the moment that Mr Clegg, after a theatrical show of mock offence, readily agreed to forgive and forget. The love-in was complete. Despite the bonhomie however, it is still unclear what the millions who voted for them as independent party leaders will make of their extraordinary political union, hailed by Mr Cameron as a 'historic and seismic shift' in politics. The new Prime Minister

Turn to Page 2

68-PAGE NEWSPAPER PLUS THE UNIQUE 20-PAGE *Viewspaper*

www.independent.co.uk
THURSDAY 13 MAY 2010
number 7,358

THE INDEPENDENT

SINCE 1986 FREE FROM PARTY-POLITICAL TIES | FREE FROM PROPRIETORIAL INFLUENCE

I, Nick, take you, Dave, to be my leader...

...for better, for worse...

Dave and Nick, Britain's new power couple

....for richer, for poorer...

...in sickness and in health...

...till debt us do part.

THE TIMES

Max 14C, min 1C
Thursday May 13 2010 timesonline.co.uk No 69946
£1

the table — Why it's never too cold to barbecue

Nick Clegg makes to leave and David Cameron pulls a comic grimace after being reminded that he once replied "Nick Clegg" when asked for his favourite joke. The pair have promised grown-up government

A very British revolution

Cameron and Clegg pledge to serve five years together

Roland Watson Political Editor

David Cameron and Nick Clegg introduced Britain to a radical new political landscape yesterday as they committed their parties to a five-year marriage of consensual government.

The Prime Minister and the Deputy Prime Minister ushered in an era of "new politics", promising a stable and durable coalition to take the country in an "historic new direction".

The scale of their revolution became clear as the Conservative and Liberal Democrat leaders staged a remarkable show of jovial but determined unity in the Downing Street rose garden. Fresh from handing five Cabinet jobs to Lib Dems, including two key economic portfolios, and planning to give Mr Clegg a minister in every department, Mr Cameron vowed to place the national interest above party interest and co-operation above confrontation.

"Compromise, give and take, reasonable, civilised, grown-up behaviour is not a sign of weakness but a sign of strength," he said.

Mr Clegg said that there would be "bumps and scrapes" along the way as two parties with different instincts joined themselves at the hip for an experiment that risks angering right-wing Tories and left-wing Liberal Democrats. He added that both leaders had taken "big risks" in going into full-blown coalition, but he insisted: "This is a government that will last."

Yet in the May sunshine, on resplendent Downing Street lawns, an improbable lightness accompanied the serious business of turning Britain around. At times, the pair were refreshingly self-deprecating. Mr Cameron pulling a comic grimace and Mr Clegg making to walk off as a journalist reminded them that the Tory leader had once answered "Nick Clegg" when asked for his favourite political joke.

The image of the pair setting up a vast tent in the centre ground of British politics poses a serious question for Labour, for which David Miliband, the former Foreign Secretary, launched his leadership campaign.

The Lib-Con arrangement rewrites the Westminster rulebook and means the previously unimaginable becoming commonplace: Mr Clegg will stand in for Mr Cameron at Prime Minister's Questions if he is away; and a Tory chief whip will demand discipline from Liberal Democrat MPs.

But some issues will test Mr Cameron's definition of grown-up government. Collective Cabinet responsibility will have to be suspended over some

Continued on page 6, col 1

Bring me sunshine
Ann Treneman's Political Sketch
page 6

IN THE NEWS

Lone survivor
A young Dutch boy was the only survivor of a plane crash in which more than 100 people, including two Britons, died on landing in Libya. The pilot had made a distress call shortly before the crash. News, page 3

Bank welcomes cuts
Mervyn King overcame his usual reticence to discuss fiscal policy to give his enthusiastic blessing to the new Government's plan to cut public spending by £6 billion immediately. Business, page 43

Oil spill tax plan
Oil companies face an immediate tax rise of 1 cent per barrel to help to pay for the clean-up in the Gulf of Mexico under proposed legislation rushed out by the White House. World, page 35

Girl accuses boys, 10
An eight-year-old girl cuddled a teddy bear as she told the Old Bailey that she was raped by two ten-year-old boys. She said that they refused to return her scooter unless she did as they wished. News, page 9

Gallant Fulham fall
Fulham's epic journey to their first European final ended in disappointment when they lost 2-1 to Atletico Madrid in extra time. Diego Forlán scored both Atletico's goals — the winner in the 116th minute. Sport, page 92

The grandma who became a hip DJ
times2life, page 17

On The Face Of It   London Underground   May 11

Laws passed in France prohibiting the wearing of the burqa brought the issue of the veil to the fore. European statistics broadly support the French stance but with many liberals paying lip service to the wearer's rights, one suspects that the dislike of the veil is more widespread. Enlightened Muslims are quick to point out that the veil has nothing to do with the Islamic religion.

In Europe, nothing could be more alien to the long and hard fought struggle to establish the rights and freedoms of the individual than for a human being to publicly deny their identity as an individual. The fact that only women wear the veil is a gratuitous insult to all women who witness a woman unidentified in this way. And it's not as if European societies do not already have laws about what citizens may wear, for example, restrictions on being naked in public.

If the objective is modesty, then by so drawing attention to themselves, the opposite effect is achieved. The way to be modest is to be invisible within the normal dress code of a culture. Those women who wear the veil assert their right to dress as they wish and President Obama has opined that : 'Western societies should not dictate what Muslim women wear'.

The assertion of any right immediately carries with it the obligation to extend that same right to all others, reciprocally as in : 'Muslim societies should not dictate what Western women wear', and universally as in : 'Should any society anywhere dictate what women wear?'

An exact illustration of this issue occurred in August 2010 at the five-star Dubai Shopping Mall :

A British woman was buying clothes and gifts, fully clothed but in a low cut top, when she was accosted by a local woman who criticised her for wearing 'revealing clothing' ; the pair then became embroiled in a heated row in front of bemused shoppers. Incensed by the Arabic woman's comments, the British woman told her to 'mind her own business' before stripping down to her bikini and walking around the Mall, taunting the locals. The Mall's security team intervened, arrested the British holidaymaker and took her to a police station, before releasing her later in the day.

The Mall, near to hotels with swimming pools, has signs asking shoppers to dress modestly, although Westerners routinely ignore the advisories. The British Foreign Office website advises visitors to the UAE : 'You should respect local traditions, customs, laws, and religion and be aware of your actions to ensure that they do not offend other cultures or religious beliefs. Women should dress modestly when in public areas, such as shopping malls. Clothes should cover the tops of the arms and legs, and underwear should not be visible'.

117

Bored with life? Things going round in circles?

Proceed directly to the next Hay Festival, it will pump adrenalin into every

intellectual cell of your body and leave you buzzing with ideas and energy.

The Inspiration Of Hay   Hay on Wye, Hereford   May 30

The Inspiration Of Hay

Hay on Wye, Hereford

May 30

Summer   Whitesand Bay, Pembroke   May 31

Touching The Wild   Whitesand Bay, Pembroke   May 31

Poetry Garden Party   Withington, Manchester   June 20

june

North of England poet, Clare Shaw performing in the
Village Hall at the Poetry Garden Party.

Poets ... Village Hall, Didsbury, Manchester June 20

... and Players   Poetry Garden Party, Didsbury, Manchester   June 20

Chris Davies on Tabla, Matthew Halsall on Trumpet

What one person can do

Linda Chase, an American in England, a Poet, Tai Chi teacher
and social axis mundi, inspired, motivated and mothered
a generation of artists, poets and otherwise lonesome souls
before being taken away by breast cancer in early 2011.
Though no one knew it at the time, very sadly, the 2010 Poetry
Garden Party proved to be her last. For the last thirty years,
whether at her large rambling Victorian house or through the
extensive cultural programme at the Village Hall in the
grounds, Linda made an exemplary contribution to the social
life of Manchester, deeply touching the hearts of many of those
with whom she came in contact.

Pic - Garth Williams

Poet Laureate   Poetry Garden Party, Didsbury, Manchester   June 20

Carol Ann Duffy, our much loved Poet Laureate, makes a wonderful poetic offering to the
Poets and Players fundraising event organised by Linda Chase,
(in the middle with red hair and turquoise top).

Hospitality   Wimbledon, London   June 22

Merchandise   Wimbledon, London   June 22

As usual a sell out for months in advance and hosting 489,000 people over the two weeks, the 2010 Wimbledon was noteworthy for the extraordinary first round match between American John Isner and Frenchman Nicolas Mahut. Suspended for bad light later on the evening of June 22, lasting all day the next day until again suspended for bad light and going into a third day for another 65 minutes, the final set ended up 68-70 in Isner's favour (6-4, 3-6, 6-7, 7-6, 70-68). In so doing it broke numerous tennis match records:

- Longest match - 11 hrs 5 mins
- The longest play in a single day
- Most games in a match - 183
- Longest set - fifth set - 8 hrs 11 mins
- Fifth set alone was 90 mins longer than the previous longest match

- Most games in a set -138 in the fifth set
- Total aces in a match - 216
- Most aces in a match by one player - Isner 113
- Second highest number of aces in a match - Mahut 103
- Consecutive service games held (168: 84 for each player)

Fired Up   Wimbledon, London   June 22

The crowds disperse on a very hot June day. Andy Murray, Britain's best tennis player for the last 50 years though not on his preferred surface on grass, had beaten Jan Hajek earlier on and progressed to the semi finals where he met an in form Rafael Nadal. Nadal retained the Men's Singles Title, Serena Williams the Women's Singles Title.

The Queen   Castlefields, Manchester   June 23

Gathered for England's crunch World Cup qualifying match against
Slovenia, the crowd give a rousing rendition of the National Anthem :

God save our gracious Queen,
Long live our noble Queen,
God save the Queen:
Send her victorious,
Happy and glorious,
Long to reign over us:
God save the Queen.

The Goal   Castlefields, Manchester   June 23

Jermaine Defoe snaps up a sharp chance for the only goal of the match.

The England Football Supporter Position   Castlefields, Manchester   June 23

WAGS Unimpressed   Castlefields, Manchester   June 23

Qualification   Castlefields, Manchester   June 23

England squeezed through against the much lesser soccer nation of Slovenia, thereby avoiding the dishonour of not making it out of the qualifying group, a fate that befell Italy, France and Nigeria leading to national torment (Italy) world cup squad bust ups (France) and the suspension of the national team and direct rule by Central Government (Nigeria).

The English football team was widely slated for its lacklustre, lethargic and uninspiring style of play and its celebrations were short lived. A few days later, they were dumped out of the tournament, losing 2 - 4 * to a younger, quicker witted, more athletic and tactically astute German side.

* There were two rule changing incidents in the 2010 World Cup:

Trailing 1-2 to Germany towards half time, England suffered one of the worst refereeing decisions in World Cup history, when Frank Lampard's equalizer bounced off the underside of the crossbar two metres beyond the goal line but was not called a goal, hence the above scoreline of 2-4 even though the official scoreline was 1-4. How can FIFA not bring in goal line technology after such a huge embarrassment?

The other rule changing incident concerned the Uruguayan striker Luis Suarez, whose deliberate handball on the goal line agonizingly denied Ghana their rightful place as Africa's first World Cup semi-finalists - genuine football supporters worldwide were outraged. In the first few months of the 2010/11 English Premier League, from 40 penalties taken by the 10 sides awarded the most penalties, only 29 resulted in goals - a failure rate of 27%. Suarez obviously knew such odds and decided the risk of being sent off and suspended was worth taking. Ghana missed the resultant penalty and then lost the subsequent penalty shoot out after extra time. Surely FIFA must bring in the 'Penalty Goal' to prevent such blatant and cynical gamesmanship?

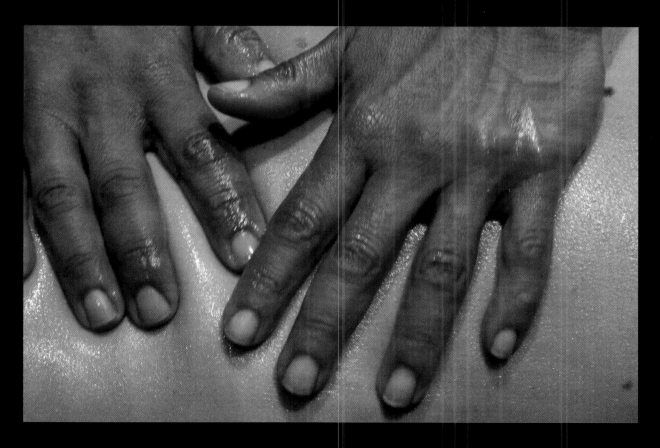

Ayurvedic Massage　　　　　　　　　Brighton, Sussex　　　　　　　　　July 23

july

Mahatma Gandhi

Tavistock Square, London

July 07

Mahatma Gandhi, the supreme advocate of non violent resistance,
meditates quietly in the centre of Tavistock Square :
"There are many causes that I am prepared to die for
but no causes that I am prepared to kill for."

With great poignancy, the 7/7 bus bomb exploded a short distance away on
the other side of Tavistock Square, killing 13 people and injuring 110 others.

7 / 7 Memorial   Hyde Park, London   July 07

Paul Mourns   Hyde Park, London   July 07

To the memory of those who
died on 7/7 2005.
This city will never forget
you.
Boris Johnson
MAYOR OF LONDON

From the
grateful mother
of a survivor

London Mourns   Hyde Park, London   July 07

139

The last thing anyone should do in Britain is to offend the Rain Gods by suggesting that we're not having enough rain - they really do seem to take the matter rather personally. In the great drought of 1976, the Sikh community in Southall flew in from the Punjab, loincloth n'all, a traditional Indian rainmaker. After the holy man meditated deeply, it started raining within a week and it didn't really stop raining for the next 18 months - a great spiritual victory that the Sikh community rightfully claims for itself.

After the driest start of the year in the North West since records began in 1929, a hose pipe ban was introduced on July 07. Needless to say, this senseless provocation led to an immediate flexing of the divine muscles. ' Following significant rainfall in July and August ' (it tonked it down mercilessly), the hosepipe ban rapidly became redundant, being lifted on August 20.

The Rain Gods   Dovestone Reservoir, Peak District   July 13

Fecundity   St Andrews, Fife   July 17

Strawberry Pickers   Arbroath, Angus   July 18

Fertility   Howe Of Fife   July 18

From The Far East   The Open, St Andrews   July 18

From Down Under   The Open, St Andrews   July 18

The Swilcan Bridge 18th Hole, St Andrews July 18

Dating back over 700 years to a shepherd's bridge over a small burn, the Swilcan Bridge is one of golf's most iconic images and many famous golfers and celebrities have been photographed on it.

Late on the Friday evening of the 2010 tournament, the 60 year old American Tom Watson, 5 times Open Champion and in his last Open at St Andrews, thought fit to bid farewell to the oldest golf course in the world, by kissing the hallowed stones and waving to the crowds - soaking it all in, just as his old friends and rivals Arnold Palmer and Jack Nicklaus had done before him:

'It just seemed the right thing to do' Watson said 'I thought of Arnold on the bridge and Jack on the bridge. Their last Opens were right here at St Andrews.'

Tom Morris   18th Hole, St Andrews   July 18

TOM MORRIS AND TOMMY MORRIS

TOM MORRIS (1821-1908) LIVED IN THIS HOUSE FROM 1866 UNTIL HIS DEATH IN 1908. MORRIS WON THE OPEN CHAMPIONSHIP FOUR TIMES (1861, 1862, 1864 AND 1867). HE WAS KEEPER OF THE GREEN IN St. ANDREWS FROM 1864 UNTIL 1903. HIS SON, TOMMY, WHO ALSO WON THE OPEN CHAMPIONSHIP FOUR TIMES (1868, 1869, 1870 AND 1872), LIVED IN THIS HOUSE FROM 1866 UNTIL 1874 AND THEN AGAIN IN 1875 UNTIL HIS DEATH HERE ON 25TH DECEMBER THAT YEAR.

The 150th anniversary of The Open at St Andrews was marked by a stiff breeze that blew throughout the last three days. The only player whose technique mastered the tricky conditions was the South African, Louis Oosthuizen who at 16 under went on to win his first major title by a wide margin, seven shots clear of the field.

This continued the trend for 'one off wonders' to have won one of golf's four major titles only once. Out of the 40 major titles in a decade, there were 12 'one off wonders' in the 1990s, increasing to 18 out of the 40 in the 2000s. Louis Oosthuizen missed the cut on the four majors before St Andrews and on the two majors following his 2010 Open victory.

Louis Oosthuizen   Open Champion, St Andrews   July 18

English Summer

Brighton, Sussex

July 22

Evening Cool   Brighton, Sussex   July 22

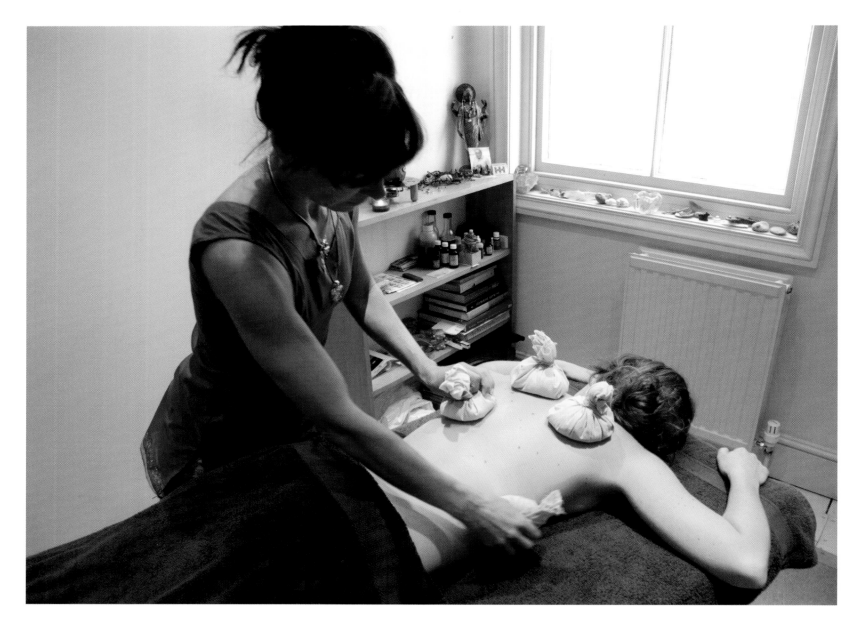

Ayurveda   Brighton, Sussex   July 23

Derived from Ayus (longevity) and Vedas (knowledge), and literally meaning the science of longevity, Ayurvedic medicine is the ancient system of Indian medicine that can trace its source knowledge back 3,000-4,000 years.

Considered in the West as complementing rather than replacing Western medicine, Ayurveda is a comprehensive system of medicine in its own right.

Grounded in the metaphysics of the Sacred Elements (Earth, Water, Fire, Air, Space), body, mind and spirit/consciousness need to be addressed to ensure vitality and health.

Micha Augustin, the practitioner above, uses hot pouches to work on the "marma points", similar to the pressure points in reflexology, acupuncture and acupressure.

Brighton itself has for some time been established as a centre for alternative cultures and in the May 2010 General Election, perhaps not surprisingly, it had the distinction of electing Caroline Lucas as Britain's first Green MP.

The Sound Of The Sea   Brighton, Sussex   July 22

Magna Carta, 1215   Runnymede, Surrey   July 23

Derived from the Anglo Saxon, 'runieg' (regular meeting) and 'mede' (meadow) and normally held in the open air, the itinerant Witanagemot meetings of Anglo Saxon potentates (625-1066) would gather from time to time at Runnymede during the reign of Alfred The Great.

Looking much the same today as it did then, it is not hard to imagine the gathering of powerful men with their private armies, tents and horses that imposed themselves on the hapless King John at Runnymede in the June of 1215.

Although it would take the rest of the 13th century to fully consolidate the charter of 1215, and although the Magna Carta was part of a much broader historical process, the crucial thing was that, for the first time, it placed the English monarch firmly under the Rule of Law.

No English King could act in a whimsical or tyrannical manner to erode the rights of free men, (Articles 39 & 40), nor could the King dominate the Church (Article 1). The liberties of towns, ports and cities were guaranteed and merchants of all nations were allowed free passage. (Articles13 & 41). In addition, the rights of widows to refuse to be re-married were recognised, as were consumer rights through the proclamation of a rudimentary principle of national weights and measures.

It is on Articles 39 and 40 that most historical emphasis has been placed :

39. No freeman shall be arrested, imprisoned or disseised or outlawed or exiled or in any way destroyed. Nor will we go upon him, nor send upon him, except by the lawful judgement of his peers or by the law of the land.

40. To no one will we sell, to no one will we refuse or delay, right or justice.

Although Magna Carta in the medieval period did not in general limit the power of kings, by the time of the English Civil War, it had become an important symbol for those who wished to show that the King was bound by the law. It influenced the early settlers in New England and, through the codification of 'due process under Law', it lies at the foundation of the world's oldest written constitution, that of the United States; ultimately leading to the Universal Declaration of Human Rights in 1948, (Articles 6 -12).

We Shall Pay Any Price

Runnymede, Surrey

July 23

Let every nation know, whether it wishes us well or ill, that we shall pay any price, bear any burden, meet any hardship, support any friend or oppose any foe, in order to ensure the survival and success of liberty. (President Kennedy - Inaugural Address - January 20, 1961)

American Bar Monument

At its monument at Runnymede, the American legal profession regularly commemorates and reaffirms its faith in the principle of the Rule of Law.

Hollyhocks   Brighton Pavillion, Sussex   July 23

Royal Horticultural Society   Tatton Park, Knutsford, Cheshire   July 24

Cottage Garden Society   Tatton Park, Knutsford, Cheshire   July 24

Chrysanthemums   Tatton Park, Knutsford, Cheshire   July 24

HMS Richmond   Navy Days, Portsmouth   July 30

4.5 inch Mark 8 Naval Gun   Navy Days, Portsmouth   July 30

HMS Cumberland   Navy Days, Portsmouth   July 30

Extreme Sailing Series I   Cowes Week, Isle of Wight   July 31

In 1826, seven yachts under the flag of the Royal Yacht Club raced for a gold cup worth £100. The following year, King George IV presented the King's Cup and, except during the two world wars, yacht racing has taken place at Cowes every year since then, making it the world's longest running regatta. 250-300 yacht races now take place over eight days with 8,000-9,000 competitors.

Starting out as a traditional three day yachting regatta, it quickly became part of the social calendar, eventually developing into the modern 'Cowes Week', attracting 100,000 visitors to the festive atmosphere of a major sports event with an extensive arts programme. Though a few events still preserve its elite billing, Cowes Week otherwise brings the sport of sailing and many other water based activities to a wide variety of people from all walks of life.

Egypt Point   Cowes Week, Isle of Wight   July 31

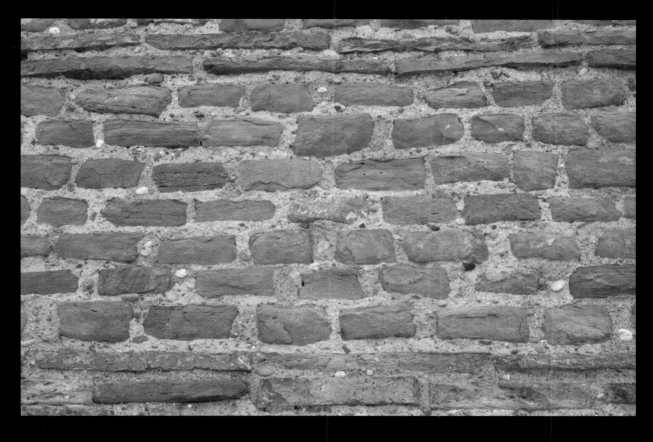

Roman Wall   Wroxeter, Shropshire   Aug 07

august

At its peak, the 2nd Century AD Roman town of Virconium (SE of present day Shrewsbury) was the fourth largest Roman settlement in Britain with a population of about 15,000. The remnants of the public baths complex is mostly what remains, along with the large wall that separated the baths from the exercise hall in the heart of the city.

More prosaically, it is hard to think of Britain having hordes of Italians beautifying themselves without it having a direct impact on the British gene pool - all that hirsute warrior beast stuff didn't always cut it with the ladies. One imagines that the genetic inheritance of Britain rather resembles the origins of the English language - our genes, like our words, have come from everywhere.

Roman Baths   Viroconium / Wroxeter   Shropshire   Aug 07

Pilae - part of the underfloor heating system of Roman baths. Supporting a stone slab floor sitting on top of the pilae, the stacks of brick tiles allowed for hot air to be blown underneath.

With some fine medieval and Georgian buildings in its historic centre, the charming market town of Ludlow is typical of many dozens of small to medium sized market towns dotted all over the British countryside. They add great character to our way of life and serve as a timely correction to the prevailing metaphor of Britain as urban, intensely populated and socially alienated.

Town House   Ludlow, Shropshire   Aug 07

Olde England   Ludlow, Shropshire   Aug 07

The Moors   Above Mytholmroyd. W Yorkshire   Aug 14

Solid Rock   Heptonstall, W Yorkshire   Aug 14

Stone Town   Haworth, W Yorkshire   Aug 14

Founded in 1887 as Haworth Wesleyan Cricket Club, then as Haworth Methodist CC and now known as Haworth CC, the club nestles in the picturesque hillsides of the Worth Valley, a quarter of a mile away from Charlotte Bronte's Parsonage.

At the time of this match, against Oakworth CC, Haworth found itself running out of games and perilously placed near the drop zone in Division One of the Craven & District Cricket League. Batting first, Haworth were bowled out for 107 - a relatively easy target for the opposition. Coasting to victory earlier in their innings, in the end, Oakworth just scrambled home at 109-9.

It was not until Haworth came out on top of a vital bottom of the table clash two weeks later against Ingrow CC, that they secured their place in Division One with a more assured 6 wicket win.

Clean Bowled   Haworth Cricket Club, W Yorkshire   Aug 14

Caught On The Boundary   Haworth Cricket Club, W Yorkshire   Aug 14

Straight Down The Wicket

Lord's, London

Aug 26

Rain Stopped Play   Lord's, London   Aug 26

Corruption Stopped Play

The Lords test of 2010 was completely marred by 'spot fixing' allegations against three members of the Pakistani team and their agent. Unusual betting patterns surrounded the bowling of deliberate no balls, and this was picked up by a journalistic sting operation by the News of the World. It eventually led to 5 year bans on playing cricket being served on Salman Butt, Mohammad Asif and Mohammad Amir. These three cricketers also face further police charges of corruption in London's Marleybone Magistrates Court.

As for the match itself, not surprisingly Pakistan slumped to defeat by a huge margin of an innings and 225 runs, their worst ever Test defeat.

All The World's A Stage   Globe Theatre, London   Aug 26

Shakespeare at The Globe - one of the outstanding things to do in London.
And at £5 per ticket standing in 'The Yard, also one of the cheapest.

Sue's Rings   Chiswick, London   Aug 26

Sue's Things   Chiswick, London   Aug 26

Sue's Sound System   Chiswick, London   Aug 26

Calling The Spirits   Chiswick, London

Semi professional musician, Sue Shorter bears fulsome witness to the fact that the cult
of the British eccentric is not only confined to the male of the species.

Merely Players   Globe Theatre, London   Aug 26

Flint Cobbled   Blakeney, Norfolk   Aug 27

Salt Marsh   Blakeney, Norfolk   Aug 27

Caravan Park   Skegness, Lincolnshire   Aug 27

Holiday Pub   Skegness, Lincolnshire   Aug 27

Caravan Suburbia   Skegness, Lincolnshire   Aug 27

Away   Skegness, Lincolnshire   Aug 27

Union   Moneymore, Co. Londonderry   Aug 29

Closing Time   Mahon's Hotel, Irvinestown, Co Fermanagh   Aug 29

The Troubles   Belleek, Co Fermanagh   Aug 30

The Talking   Belleek, Co Fermanagh   Aug 30

High School For Girls   Enniskillen, Co Fermanagh   Aug 30

All the girls at the Collegiate Grammar School are Protestant.

High School For Girls   Enniskillen, Co Fermanagh   Aug 30

All the girls at the Mount Lourdes Grammar School are Catholic.

In the 4th - 5th century Caldragh graveyard on Boa Island in Lough Erne, this primitive, enigmatic double headed stone figure evokes the Celtic roots of pre-Christian Ireland. Thought to represent a Celtic deity, it may have been used by early Christians who included older pagan beliefs in their grave sites. Though not specifically representing Janus, the stone takes its name from the Roman two headed deity of that name.

The Janus Stone   Boa Island, Co. Fermanagh   Aug 30

Lough Erne   Co. Fermanagh   Aug 30

After beautifying themselves at the nearby Roman baths at Cilurnum, the average Roman soldier must have stared forlornly northwards at a bleak landscape of rain, bog, swamp and forest - after all they were Italian. Azure blue coastlines, warm sunshine, sensuous women and rich Mediterranean cooking cannot have been far from their thoughts - it must have been the modern day equivalent of being posted to North Korea or Somalia.

Not entirely without foundation (as anyone who has ever encountered a drunken Scotsman can testify), the Romans must have taken one look at Scotland, one look at the Picts and Scots and concluded that that's where the known world should end. Beyond that lay something they knew they could never comprehend.

Fortress   Vercovicium, Hadrian's Wall, Northumbria   Aug 31

The Wall   Hadrian's Wall, Northumbria   Aug 31

Forest Floor   Crickley Hill, Gloucestershire   Sept 26

september

Snack   St Anne's Square, Manchester   Sept 04

'Snack', originating from the Middle Dutch word ' snacken' meaning to bite, itself
a variant of 'snappen' meaning to snap and used in this sense in Middle English
from the 1300s. It eventually entered usage as an item of food in the 1600s.

Bravo The Eighth Day! Their website describes its origins from the proverbial bunch of hippies in the 1960s : 'As the Sixties rushed to a psychedelic close with a blaze of love and chemicals heralding the dawn of a New Age, a right-on group of friends had their stab at creating a new order. They wanted to establish a way of trading goods that broke away from the ideas of money commerce and to that end founded On The Eighth Day.

During the first six years the business was run as a co-operative but was in fact legally a partnership. In 1976 On the Eighth Day Co-operative Limited registered as a workers' co-operative under the Provident Societies Act. This means that most of the full time workers in the business become members of the co-operative, currently twelve, and both work and manage the business. These days we have to be business-like to survive but still have a place for ethics. Our food is still vegetarian, we try to be as 'green' as possible, we are still involved in striving towards a better world and our wages are still unfortunately crap.'

Health Food   Oxford Road, Manchester   Sept 02

Vegetarian Co-op   Oxford Road, Manchester   Sept 02

Bazaar   Rusholme, Manchester   Sept 02

So ingrained into the British way of life has the curry become that one could well imagine extreme right wing members of the BNP ranting about immigration, whilst scoffing a gut igniting curry from the local Indian take away.

With its continual buzz of activity and with its fun 'see and be seen' atmosphere, Rusholme in Manchester is, arguably, the most convincing curry mile in Britain.

Curry Mile   Rusholme, Manchester   **Sept 02**

Staircase Locks   Foxton, Leicestershire   Sept 17

Unlocked   Foxton, Leicestershire   Sept 17

The Old School   King's School, Grantham, Lincolnshire   Sept 17

The Apple Tree   Woolsthorpe Manor, Colsterworth, Lincolnshire   Sept 17

Now the school library, the Old School building at King's School in Grantham was where Isaac Newton attended from 1655-1660, before going up to Trinity College, Cambridge in 1661. There he immersed himself in mathematics, the modern philosophy of Descartes and the work of the astronomers, Copernicus, Galileo and Kepler. The University closed as a precaution against the Great Plague of 1665, and, fortuitously for the cause of science, resulted in a lengthy sojourn at his birthplace at Woolsthorpe Manor. There, in private contemplation, Newton advanced his theories on calculus, optics and, famously, the law of gravitation. There, looking from his window (the upstairs room on the right of the manor house) and as recorded by his biographer Stukeley in conversation with Newton in 1726, shortly before he died :

'when formerly, the notion of gravitation came into his mind. It was occasioned by the fall of an apple, as he sat in contemplative mood. Why should that apple always descend perpendicularly to the ground, thought he to himself. Why should it not go sideways or upwards, but constantly to the Earth's centre? Assuredly the reason is, that the Earth draws it. There must be a drawing power in matter. And the sum of the drawing power in the matter of the Earth must be in the Earth's centre, not in any side of the Earth. Therefore does this apple fall perpendicularly or towards the centre? If matter thus draws matter; it must be proportion of its quantity. Therefore the apple draws the Earth, as well as the Earth draws the apple.'

Still producing apples:

'It went down very nicely'

The Scientist - Isaac Newton   Royal Society, London   Sept 18

The Real Heroes

One might read Aristotle, the Ten Commandments, the Tao Te Ching or The Prophet, and barring the odd technological clanger, they are as relevant today as they ever were. Relatively little has changed in the nature of human affairs over the last few thousand years. The people that have really changed everything in daily life have been the scientists and everyone on the planet owes them a huge debt of gratitude. They should be accorded the highest level of respect.

British culture is blessed with a natural sense of intellect and inquiry and, in this spirit in the 1640s and 1650s and despite the turmoil of the Civil War, various scientists, mathematicians & philosophers met informally in London and Oxford to discuss 'The New Philosophy' - a new way of thinking that relied on first hand observation and experiment to understand the world - and which we now call science.

Together with courtiers, clergymen, doctors, lawyers, writers and merchants, what became known as The Royal Society emerged in the early 1660s. 350 years later in 2010, the Royal Society is now a fellowship of the world's most eminent scientists and is the oldest scientific academy in continuous existence. Its list of members is the history of science.

Philosophiae Naturalis Principia Mathematica (1687)

(The Mathematical Principles of Natural Philosophy)

Perhaps the most important science book ever published, Newton's theories changed the way people understood the world. It explained the mathematical formulae governing the laws of the Universe :

Newton's law of universal gravitation states that every point mass in the universe attracts every other point mass with a force that is directly proportional to the product of their masses and inversely proportional to the square of the distance between them.

Newton's law has since been superseded by Einstein's theory of general relativity, but it continues to be used as an excellent approximation of the effects of gravity. Relativity is only required when there is a need for extreme precision, or when dealing with gravitation for extremely massive and dense objects.

Newton's Three Laws of Motion :

First Law : An object will remain at rest or in uniform motion in a straight line unless acted upon by an external force.

Second Law : When force is applied to an object, it accelerates

$F = ma$ Acceleration (a) takes place in the direction of the applied force and is proportional to the magnitude of the force (F), and is inversely proportional to the mass of the object (m).

Third Law : To every action there is always an equal and opposite reaction
If you press a stone with your finger, the finger is also pressed by the stone.

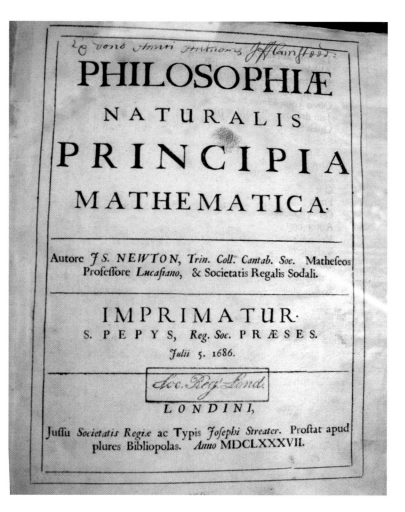

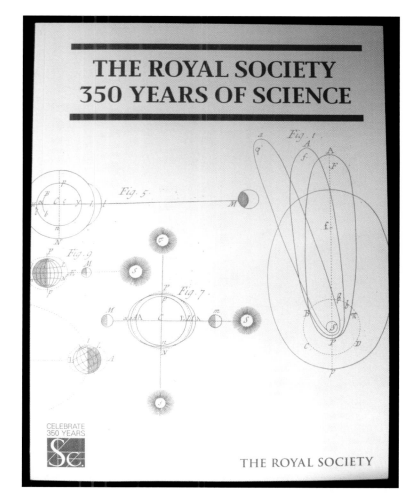

The Laws of Nature   Royal Society, London   Sept 18

Day Of Atonement For The One   The City, London   Sept 18

Outside a humble back street synagogue and wrapped in a prayer shawl
signifying the presence of God, a congregant prays devoutly on Yom
Kippur, the deepest and most meaningful day in the Jewish religious year.

Day of Atonement For The Many   The Pope, Westminster Cathedral, London   Sept 18

'Here, too, I think of the immense suffering caused by the abuse of children, especially within the Church and by her ministers. Above all, I express my deep sorrow to the innocent victims of these unspeakable crimes, along with my hope that the power of Christ's grace, his sacrifice of reconciliation, will bring deep healing and peace to their lives. I also acknowledge with you the shame and humiliation which all of us have suffered because of these sins; and I invite you to offer it to the Lord with trust that this chastisement will contribute to the healing of victims, the purification of the Church and the renewal of her age-old commitment to the education and care of young people. I express my gratitude for the efforts being made to address this problem responsibly, and I ask all of you to show your concern for the victims and solidarity with your priests.'

Papal Address - Westminster Cathedral - Sept 18

Black Swan   Slimbridge, Gloucestershire   Sept 26

Otters   Slimbridge, Gloucestershire   Sept 26

The Wildfowl & Wetlands Trust is a conservation charity with nine reserves and visitor centres throughout Britain, home to over 150,000 birds and supported by 200,000 members and over one million visitors per year.

Founded at Slimbridge in 1946 by the late Sir Peter Scott, ornithologist, artist and the voice of Natural History broadcasting in Britain in the 50s, 60s and 70s. The only son of the explorer 'Scott of the Antarctic', amongst numerous distinctions, Peter Scott was a founder member of the WWF and designer of its panda logo.

Pink Flamingo   Slimbridge, Gloucestershire   Sept 26

The Power Of Nature   Crickley Hill, Gloucestershire   Sept 26

The Druids Prayer

Ancestors, grant us your Protection

And in Protection, Strength

And in Strength, Understanding

And in Understanding, Knowledge

And in Knowledge, Knowledge of Justice

And in the Knowledge of Justice, the Love of it,

And in the Love of it, the Love of all existences,

And in the Love of all existences,

The love of the Ancestors and all things good.

So may it be.

The Way Of Nature   Crickley Hill, Gloucestershire   Sept 26

Cotswold Order of Druids, Autumnal Equinox

Ceremonies for the eight pagan festivals each year, both now and in the past, were for local communities to come together and pay homage to the earth for her provisions and to the heavens, for the sun, the wind and the rain.

Above   Hughtown, Scilly Isles   Sept 27

Below   Hughtown, Scilly Isles   Sept 27

South   St Agnes, Scilly Isles   Sept 27

There's something special about the Scilly Isles ..... intimate, friendly, very much on a human scale and a glimpse into what Britain used to be like, a Britain where trust, decency and mutual respect hold sway. Consciously or unconsciously, all visitors partake of the elevated status of being at the very end of the line. Location, location, location in its spiritual sense.

Motor launches leave Hughtown in the mornings for short journeys to the outlying islands. No cars, no roads, gentle hiking, striking rock scenery, gallons of fresh Atlantic air and impossibly tranquil ...

Fresh Air   St Agnes, Scilly Isles   Sept 27

Workshop   Hughtown, Scilly Isles   Sept 28

Sailmaker   Hughtown, Scilly Isles   Sept 28

Keith Buchanan, an all round 'go for it guy', originally came to the Scilly
Isles for water sports as a 19 year old, opened and ran a successful sailing
school, initiated and passed on various boat businesses, now a hotelier,
boat builder, canvas products and sailmaker - truly, a life well lived.

Clay   Eleanor Newell, Potter   Lamorna, Cornwall   Sept 29

Clay Pit   Eden Project, Cornwall   Sept 29

225

The Potter's Wheel   Eleanor Newell, Potter   Lamorna, Cornwall   Sept 29

"From the preparation of materials through to scrubbing clean the final pieces, all my senses are fully engaged. I am constantly in awe of the limitless possibilities of clay available to me as an artist."

Eleanor Newell, an acclaimed expert in Raku pottery, at work in Lamorna near Penzance. Originating in tea ceremony bowl making in Japan in the 1600s and subsequently introduced by the famous British potter, Bernard Leach, at his studio in St Ives in the 1920s, the Raku style has expanded to become a creative process whereby the skilful variation of temperature, timing, clay mix and glaze ensures that almost every piece is unique, a work of art.

The Celtic Wheel of the Year has eight spokes which connects it to the eight major divisions
of the Celtic year - the longest and shortest day and the two equinoxes (the four Albans),
and Samhain, Brigantia, Beltane and Lugnassadh (the four Fire Festivals).
The Albans are the oldest, which is why some older wheels have only four spokes.

The Celtic Wheel   Eden Project, Cornwall   Sept 29

Many influences must have converged to provide the creative force behind the highly imaginative Eden Project but it is hard to escape the power of place, which leads directly to Cornwall's distinct identity and its Celtic roots - Cornwall has always felt different.

Indeed, Tim Smit, co-founder of the Eden Project, has been vocal in his support of the huge copper clad Celtic Cross to be installed in 2012 at Saltash, upon crossing the River Tamar into Cornwall, the Tamar having been the western boundary of both Roman and Anglo Saxon Britain. Across that historic boundary, and for 1,500 years before the imposition of the

Norman conquest, Cornwall formed part of the wider Celtic culture that flourished from Scotland, Wales and Ireland through to Brittany, and through trade routes to the South of France and into Eastern Europe.

With its spectacular coastal scenery generating an innate sense of liberation, Cornwall's strong force is its connection with Nature. This spaciousness has always been a magnet for artists and crafts people, and the creative industries are a major element in present day Cornish culture. It was from this background that the Eden Project emerged, gained support and transformed a grubby clay pit into an inspiring work of natural creation.

Human Creation   Eleanor Newell, Potter   Lamorna, Cornwall   Sept 29

Natural Creation   Eden Project, Cornwall   Sept 29

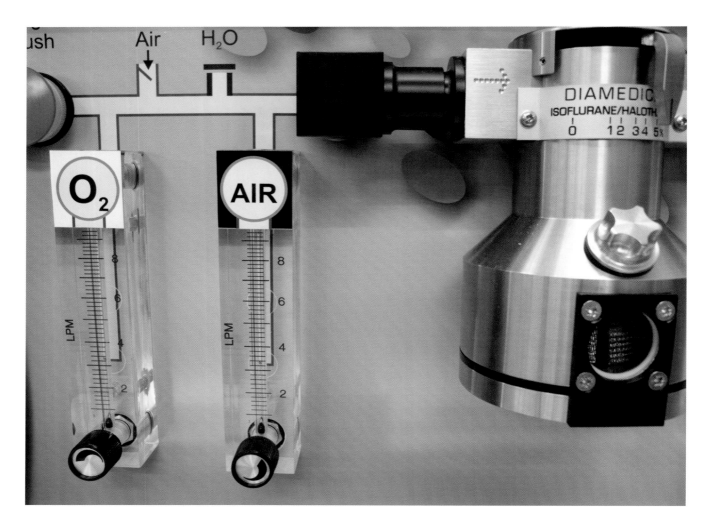

Life Saver   Bratton Fleming, Devon   Sept 30

Portable Life   Bratton Fleming, Devon   Sept 30

Anaesthesia   Bratton Fleming, Devon   Sept 30

Despite the West's best of intentions, aid to the Third World has resulted in piles of high tech junk that's far too complex to operate and that can't be maintained when it breaks down. The World Health Organisation estimates that 70% of medical equipment supplied to developing countries fails to work. Therefore, it is most refreshing to see a fine piece of kit that exudes relevance.

Designed for use in low income countries where resources are scarce and power supplies unreliable, the Diamedica anaesthetic systems are designed to function regardless of temperature and humidity, to be economical to run and simple to maintain, and to work through interruptions to electrical or oxygen supply. For use in more challenging field situations, or in disaster or conflict zones, the portable anaesthetic system, DPA 01 is a triumph of design.

Based in an unlikely part of Britain in North Devon, and exporting their systems all over third world Africa and Asia, it is exemplary to discover that a small high tech company can make such a valid contribution.

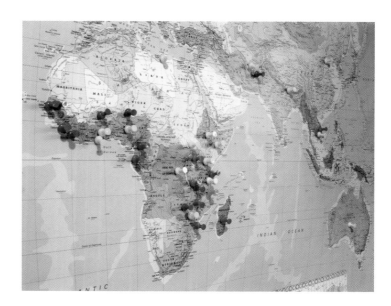

Over The Sea to Skye   NW Scotland   Oct 20

october

Autumn Cometh
Hay on Wye, Herefordshire
Oct 05

Trinity College, Oxford, sits on the original site of Durham College, founded in 1286 as a seminary for Benedictine monks from Durham Cathedral.

Trinity College itself was founded in 1555 by Sir Thomas Pope, a Catholic who had no surviving children, on land bought following the abolition of Durham College during the period of Protestant Reformation.

Academe   Trinity College, Oxford   Oct 06

Of the ten oldest universities in the world, six are in Italy : Siena, Naples, Padua, Vicenza, Modena and the oldest of all, Bologna, the word university having been coined at its foundation in 1088. Plus Cambridge, Salamanca in Spain, Coimbra in Portugal and since 1096, Oxford, the second oldest university in the world.

From its earliest days, the idea of a university was inextricably linked to the notion of academic freedom : the right of a travelling scholar to unhindered passage in the interests of education. And in 1988, on the 900th anniversary of Bologna's foundation, this was recognised in the Magna Charta Universitatum signed by 430 University Rectors worldwide.

The world's present top twenty universities are dominated by the well endowed institutions of the United States, but Oxford and Cambridge regularly feature in the top 5 or 6, normally the only non American ones in the top ten. Imperial College London and University College London are then ranked variously in the top 20 or 30.

Quadrangle   Trinity College, Oxford   Oct 06

'If you had a dream of what a proper bookshop should be,
this would be it' states Philip (Independent Oct 09).
'It's massive, stacked full of books and set within that lively
academic atmosphere that is perhaps unique to Oxford'.

Brain of Britain   Blackwells, Oxford   Oct 06

Freshers Week   Broad Street, Oxford   Oct 06

Stimulation   Blackwells, Oxford   Oct 06

1337 and all that

Edward III, Trinity College, Cambridge

Should anyone's mind glaze over trying to comprehend the history of medieval England, one need not doubt one's intellectual faculties - broadly speaking, the period has absolutely no basis in common sense.

Of the 19 Kings of England from 1066 until the Battle of Bosworth in 1485 : 4 were murdered, 4 were killed in battle, 1 was killed hunting, 2 died of 'food poisoning', 4 died early through illness and only 1 survived through to old age. Depending on exact interpretation, the Crown of England was usurped, overthrown or deposed at least 6 times over the period. For those vying for the top job, life was 'nasty, kingish and short'

One begins to get a handle on medieval kingship when one thinks of Kings as CEOs of large multinational operations, when one realises that the interminable dynastic conflicts would nowadays be dealt with by the mergers and acquisitions department at Pricewaterhouse Cooper and that the medieval boardroom was really the bedchamber - not so much a matter of ownership of the means of production, as ownership of the means of re-production. Marriages were mergers of mutual assets, wars were hostile take over bids, the Barons were the tycoons and Parliament the pension funds, continually stumping up for royal excesses of one kind or another.

None of this is to suggest that the modern day multinational chief exec's opening gambit, upon entering a high profile meeting at any top City lawyers, should be to thud a battleaxe into the conference table....... well, not literally.

Trinity College Cambridge was founded by Henry VIII in 1546 by combining the former Michaelhouse and King's Hall. The latter was started by Edward II in 1317 to provide chancery clerks for his administration, and was then formally invested by Edward III in 1337

Edward III reigned for 50 years from 1327-1377 and was widely regarded as a relatively stable and successful monarch.

He was nevertheless quick to exact revenge upon his mother, Isabella of France and her lover, Roger Mortimer, for forcing the abdication and murder of his father, Edward II. Mortimer was arrested, stripped of the land and titles he had usurped, condemned without trial and promptly hanged, drawn and quartered at Tyburn. Edward III then exiled Isabella under house arrest, permitting her to return to society after a decade or so.

Bicycles   Town Centre, Cambridge   Oct 14

Peterhouse, the oldest college in Cambridge, was founded in 1280 and has
occupied its present site since its founder Hugo de Balsham, Bishop of Ely,
purchased two houses to accommodate a Master and fourteen "worthy but
impoverished Fellows". He bequeathed 300 marks in 1286 to buy further land
to the south of St Peter's Church, on which the college's Hall was built.

Courtyard   Peterhouse, Cambridge   Oct 14

Against a background of medieval religious authoritarianism, persecution of minorities and the burgeoning
conflict between Church and State, in 1209, two clerks of Oxford University were hanged by the townsfolk
of Oxford for a murder of which they were apparently innocent. King John backed the townspeople and the
scholars of Oxford were dispersed for five years.

Some of the scholars fleeing persecution came to the newly charted and relatively prosperous market town of
Cambridge. At first they lived in lodgings in the town, but in time houses were hired as hostels with a Master
in charge of the students. By 1226 the scholars were numerous enough to have set up an organization,
represented by an official called a Chancellor and arranged regular courses of study. . From the start there
was friction between the town and the students. Students, usually aged about fourteen or fifteen, often caused
disturbances, Citizens of the town, on the other hand, were known to overcharge for rooms and food. King Henry
III took the scholars under his protection as early as 1231, arranged for them to be sheltered from exploitation by
their landlords, authorized tuition under recognized masters, and exempted the University from taxes.

Reflections   River Cam, Cambridge   Oct 14

Suilven The Awesome
Highland, Scotland
Oct 19

Cul Mor The Majestic   Highland, Scotland   Oct 19

So I cut off my hair
And I rode straight away
For the wild unknown country
Where I could not go wrong

Isis   Bob Dylan   1976

Visiting the ancient megalithic site of Callanish is as much about being there as about the power of the site itself - the sense of journey in getting to the Outer Hebrides, to the very end of Britain, to the edge of Eurasia.

The stones of local Lewisian gneiss, thought to have been erected between 2,900 BC and 2,600 BC, were covered in peat to a depth of a man's height, until the site was cleared in 1857. Since then various theories about the astronomical setting of the stones have proved inconclusive. Callanish's devotional quality is self evident so why could it not just have been a great place for a stone circle? Perhaps it reminds us of the huge span of time which separates us from our Stone Age forbears.

Stone Age   Callanish, Isle of Lewis   Oct 20

Creation   Taobh Tuath, Harris   Oct 20

Harris Tweed   Plockrapool, Harris   Oct 21

Cottage Industry   Plockrapool, Harris   Oct 21

Inlet   Plockrapool, Harris   Oct 21

Island Life   Tarbert, Harris   Oct 21

Mesmeric   Glencoe, Highland, Scotland   Oct 21

Glencoe   Highland, Scotland   Oct 21

Roji   Bridgnorth, Shropshire   Oct 25

Dr Marilyn Hammerton serving Tea in the Hammerton's traditionally styled Japanese Tea House, designed by Japanese culture specialist, Bill Tingey.

'Roji' - the poetic term used to describe the path and garden leading to the Tea House and literally meaning 'dewy ground'*. It symbolises the transition from the everyday world to the spiritual world.

'O-Cha' - the honorific term for Tea in Japanese. In English, 'The Tea' approx.

O-Cha   Bridgnorth, Shropshire   Oct 25

* ' There is no peace in the Three Worlds, they are like a house in flames.
   One emerges from the house in flames to sit on the dewy ground'
   (Lotus Sutra)

Triform   Blenheim Palace, Woodstock, Oxfordshire   Oct 25

Palazzo

Blenheim Palace, Woodstock, Oxfordshire

Oct 25

Public School   Rugby School, Rugby   Oct 25

Rugby School is the town's largest and best-known landmark and the original school stood opposite the parish church. Completed in 1574, it had its origins in the will of Lawrence Sheriff, a native of Rugby and a purveyor of spices to Queen Elizabeth I. He left land and property for the foundation of four almshouses (since demolished) and a free grammar school for the education of boys in Rugby and Brownsover. By the mid 18th century, the old school buildings were dilapidated, and the school moved to the south end of High Street. As the reputation of the school spread, it attracted students from all over the country and school fees were introduced in 1878 in what we now know as Rugby School.

Rugby School has both day and boarding-pupils, the latter in the majority. Girls have entered the sixth form since 1975 and in 1995 it went fully co-educational. The fees for day students are c.£17,000 pa and for boarders c.£27,500 pa.

Grammar School   Lawrence Sherriff School, Rugby   Oct 25

At the same time as fees were introduced, to continue Lawrence Sheriff's original intentions of free education for local boys, the Lawrence Sheriff Grammar School was founded. The Grammar School still receives a substantial proportion of its endowment income from the Lawrence Sheriff's estate every year and Rugby School continues to offer a large number of scholarship places for outstanding students from state maintained primary schools, from the local community in the immediate vicinity of Rugby.

Lawrence Sheriff School is now a mainstream state school, a selective grammar school for boys aged 11-18 serving Rugby and the surrounding area. Its buildings are owned and maintained by the Governors, its running costs are funded by the local Authority, and its Parents' Association is in the Guinness Book of Records as the UK's oldest Parents Association. In 2008 & 2010, LSS was the top performing school in the national GCSE tables. As a state-funded school, there are no fees to attend the school.

Breeze Hill School / Waterhead Roxbury Campus   Breeze Hill, Oldham   Oct 28

Prior to its makeover to form part of the new Waterhead Academy,
the former Breeze Hill Secondary School reflected the composition
of its local community and had 90-95% Asian students.

Counthill School / Waterhead Moorside Campus   Counthill, Oldham   Oct 28

Equally, the former Counthill Secondary School
reflected the composition of its local community
and had 90% white students.

The Home Office Report on the 2001 race riots in Oldham put the blame on deep rooted segregation which divided the town into No Go areas : 'they don't go to the other side of town' 'they live separate lives basically' were typically reported comments.

From September 2010, Oldham Council tackled this situation head on by integrating the students of the Counthill and Breeze Hill secondary schools into a new institution, the Waterhead Academy. It is hard to counter the viewpoint that if racial integration through education is the objective, then it is better to begin it at primary school level. Bizarrely, at the same time, Oldham is building a new Roman Catholic school. Racial division out, religious division in?

Community   Lees Road, Oldham   Oct 28

This formed part of Oldham's ambitious £266mn plan to replace all of Oldham's secondary schools. As a state of the art new high school costs c. £25mn and as Waterhead's principal David Yates described their 'iconic' new building as ' five-star hotel design with the latest technology ', Oldham Council can hardly be accused of thinking small.

Such schemes where hatched under the outgoing Labour Government's £55bn school building programme, largely axed by the incoming Conservative / Lib Dem coalition, which stopped 8 of Oldham's 13 school projects. Depending on one's views, it is debatable whether Oldham is getting it right. However it is certain that the country cannot afford it.

Residential   Counthill, Oldham   Oct 28

It might not quite match the populist qualities of the curry, but Yoga is the other main cultural import from the Indian subcontinent. With about 10,000 qualified Yoga teachers in Britain, running 2 or 3 classes per week, there are about 300,000-400,000 people doing Yoga classes every week. Say the same again who practice privately at home without attending classes, and there must be 500,000 to 750,000 people in Britain who regularly do yoga.

Hatha Yoga, the practice of yoga asanas or physical postures, is how most people in the West understand and practice Yoga. As the yoga world is indeed much obsessed with the body beautiful, the UK Office of National Statistics brackets Keep Fit and Yoga together. However, Yoga itself means Union with the Divine / God / The Self / The Universal, and the physical practice is just one of the eight limbs of Classical Yoga :

1. Yama   (universal values)
2. Niyama   (respect and observances)
3. Asana   (bodily postures)
4. Pranayama   (control of the life force)

5. Pratyahara   (withdrawal from the sense world)
6. Dharana   (concentration)
7. Dhyana   (devotional meditation)
8. Samadhi   (spiritual union and equilibrium)

Padottavirasana   Yoga Show, Olympia, London   Oct 29

To establish and maintain contact with the true innermost Self, with the ultimate reality, whilst on the one hand, every one has to find their own way and no one is ever really taught by another, on the other hand, Yoga philosophy prescribes four spiritual paths to attain this knowledge of the Self:

Karma-yoga   The path of selfless action
Bhakti-yoga   The path of love and devotion
Raja-yoga   The path of concentration and meditation
Jnana-yoga   The path of knowledge and discrimination

Each seeker is called upon to decide which yoga best corresponds to his or her natural disposition. Karma-yoga is advised for the active, bhakti-yoga for the emotional, raja-yoga for the strong-willed, and jnana-yoga for the rational. Any seeker may become established in any one of the four paths or harmonize all four of them in everyday practice. The goal of all four yogas is freedom from the assumed bondage of the mind and the realization of our true universal identity. This is what is meant by the term 'Self Realization'.

Virabhadrasana   Yoga Show, Olympia, London   Oct 29

Self Love   Yoga Show, Olympia, London   Oct 29

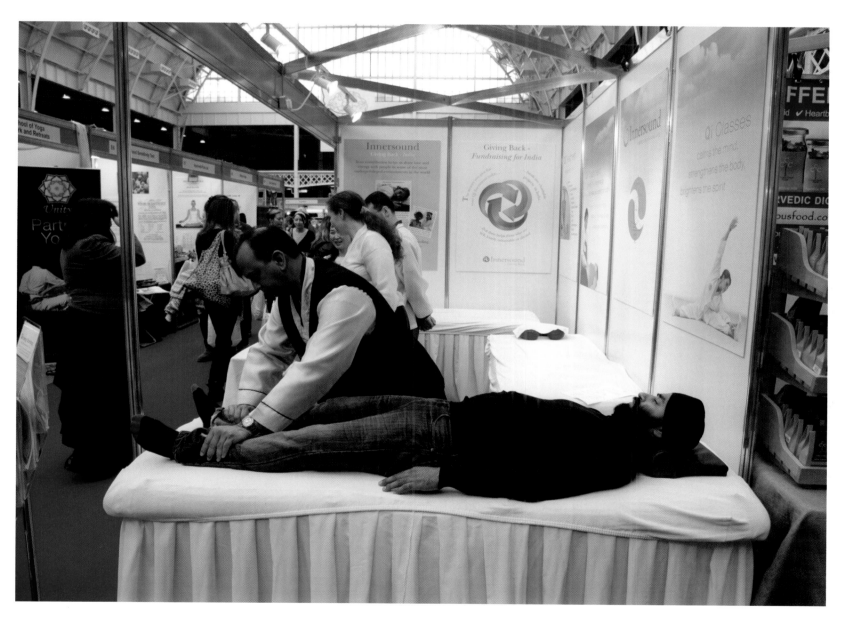

Deep Calm   Yoga Show, Olympia, London   Oct 29

Statement   Notting Hill, London   Oct 29

Display

Notting Hill, London

Oct 29

Oak Leaves   Wakefield, West Yorkshire   Nov 05

november

Since superseded by a couple of 90,000 plus square footers opened in late 2010, Sainsbury's Hedge End with 46 check outs is one of their very largest.

Megastore   Hedge End, Southampton   Nov 04

Best Fashion Street   Milsom Street, Bath, Somerset   Nov 04

Though with many familiar retail shop names, Milsom Street was voted
the best fashion street in the UK by Google Street Awards 2010.

Royal Crescent   Bath, Somerset   Nov 04

Country Pursuits   Stockbridge, Hampshire   Nov 04

Country Ladies   Stockbridge, Hampshire   Nov 04

Country High Street   Stockbridge, Hampshire   Nov 04

Fruit and Veg   Stockbridge, Hampshire   Nov 04

Fish Chowder   Stockbridge, Hampshire   Nov 04

Best Foodie Street   Stockbridge, Hampshire   Nov 04

Stockbridge High Street, voted Best Foodie Street in the UK in the 2010 Google Street Awards.
Alongside many other outlets sourcing local produce under the Hampshire Fare scheme, here
premier butchers John Robinson prepare their award winning sausages, winners of three Golds
at The Great Hampshire Sausage Competition of February 2010.

Head And Trees   Yorkshire Sculpture Park, Wakefield   Nov 05

Detail : Henry Moore - Reclining Figure, Bronze, 1985

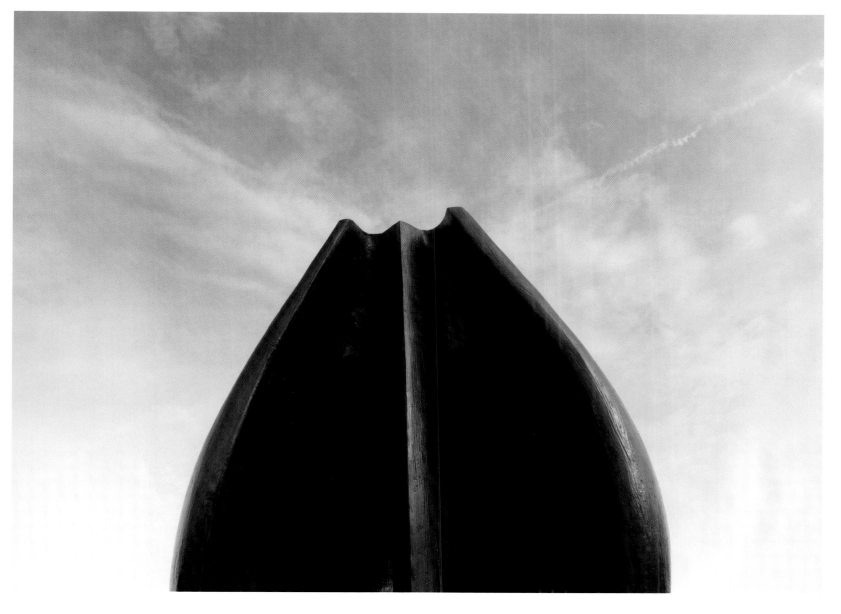

Head And Sky   Yorkshire Sculpture Park, Wakefield   Nov 05

Detail : Henry Moore - Large Totem Head, Bronze, 1968

Temple Of The Thing   Meadowhall, Sheffield   Nov 05

Things   Meadowhall, Sheffield   Nov 05

The Big Society   Miller Street, Manchester   Nov 30

The Prime Minister, David Cameron, might like to think that he's onto the latest, trendiest thing by proclaiming 'The Big Society' but the Co-operative movement got there a long time ago and has been doing Big Society for the last 150 years. Lest 'the lefties' get a bit uppity on this point, British society has of course been doing 'The Big Society' for the last few thousand years, albeit, as this publication humbly endeavours to illustrate, in a not always entirely predictable fashion.

As a matter of fact, after recent mergers with the Lothian and Plymouth Co-operatives and with United Co-operatives, after its integration with the Britannia Building Society and after the purchase of the Somerfield supermarket chain for £1.57bn, our little local friendly Co-op has now got a turnover of £14bn, 5.5 million members and 120,000 employees in 5,300 outlets. Conservatively disposed going into the 2008 financial crisis with an ethical investment stance and with loans only funded out of its own resources, The Co-operative was one of the few banks to emerge unscathed from the economic storm. The trust engendered will rebound to its advantage for many years to come.

The Bigger Society   Miller Street, Manchester   Nov 30

In July 2010, the foundation stone of its new headquarters was laid behind a hoarding that read 'The Cooperative Believes In Manchester'. One wonders whether the idea of rescuing a certain red coloured football team from megalomaniac capitalism might make the cut as one of its next ethical investments? It would certainly be the same colour as the political party it sponsors, through its extensive network of 'Labour Co-operative MPs', Lords, Assembly MPs and Local Councillors.

The Cooperative itself is merely at the head of a much more extensive co-operative movement within the UK. With 447 farming co-ops, 67 fishing co-ops and 411 workers co-ops, and including the £7.5bn turnover and 70,000 employees of the John Lewis/Waitrose/Ocado Partnership, 'The Cooperative Economy' now employs 230,000 people with a £33bn turnover, depending on how one looks at it, accounting for 1% - 2% of the British Economy.

Festive   Cavern Club, Liverpool   Dec 08

december

Big Mac   Lord Street, Liverpool   Dec 08

McDonald's opened its first restaurant in the UK in 1974 and every day more than 2.5 million people visit the present c.1,250 outlets, employing 65,000-70,000 people. McDonalds had its busiest ever month in Britain in August 2010, has had 20 quarters of successive growth and the UK business is set to expand further . The Broad Street Liverpool McDonald's is one of the largest in the UK.

Starting out life in fast food turf wars in Pittsburgh, Pennsylvania in the 1950s, the Big Mac was then rolled out across the United States in 1967. Often caricatured as a symbol of American capitalism but popular worldwide, it is used by The Economist for international price comparisons in its Big Mac Index, sometimes referred to as Burgernomics.

In 2007, McDonalds UK went Fairtrade with its coffee, sourcing it from New York based global non-profit Rainforest Alliance Certified farms . It sold 69 million cups of coffee in the UK in 2010: 'We sell more cups of coffee in the UK than Starbucks and Costa Coffee combined' (Jill McDonald, UK Chief Executive)

For anyone over 50 years of age, one of the saddest days of their lives was to hear the news on that cold grey December morning, of the murder of John Lennon in New York.

Even now, thirty years later, it is still hard to get one's head round this tragedy. One can only stare in blank incomprehension at the senseless annulment of such a truly wonderful character.

Imagine   Matthew St, Liverpool   Dec 08

The 30th Anniversary gig was performed by the excellent Liverpool based Beatles tribute band, the Blue Meanies, on this occasion, playing under the banner of John Lennon's iconic song : 'Working Class Hero'.

During the set, Jimmy Coburn (below), who has played the part of John Lennon for the last 15 years, explained how much that song meant out there in Lennon's tough, everyday Liverpool.

Working Class Hero   Cavern Club, Liverpool   Dec 08

Please Please Me
Every Little Thing
If I Fell
A Hard Day's Night
I Feel Fine
Yes It Is
And Your Bird Can Sing
This Boy
Norwegian Wood
Oh Darling
Good Morning
All You Need Is Love

The Beatles Set   Cavern Club, Liverpool   Dec 08

Strange Days Indeed
Watching The Wheels
Cold Turkey
Jealous Guy
Whatever Gets You Through The Night
Power To The People
Instant Karma
Just Like Starting Over
Happy Xmas (War Is Over)
Working Class Hero
Come Together
Imagine

The Lennon Set   Cavern Club, Liverpool   Dec 08

Off Season   Lyme Regis, Dorset   Dec 14

Winter Sky   Lyme Regis, Dorset   Dec 14

Cotswold   Poundbury, Dorset   Dec 14

Town House   Poundbury, Dorset   Dec 14

Tower   Poundbury, Dorset

It would be unfair to dub Prince Charles's urban environment project in Dorset as 'Georgian Town House meets Cotswold Village', much effort has been put into Poundbury and those interested in Town Planning should enquire further. The question is not this or that architectural style; the root issue with planning is planning itself and the constraining feeling of 'The Plan' cannot be avoided in Poundbury. One of the charms of older town environments is that of being slightly haphazard, of feeling much less totally regulated.

Georgian   Poundbury, Dorset   Dec 14

Docklands Redevelopment   Cardiff Bay, Cardiff   Dec 15

The Valleys   Merthyr Tydfil, S Wales   Dec 15

Open Cast   Ffos-y-Fran, Merthyr Tydfil, S Wales   Dec 15

Heavy Load   Ffos-y-Fran, Merthyr Tydfil, S Wales   Dec 15

Ladies That Lunch   Morlais Golf Club, Merthyr Tydfil   Dec 15

Lady Power   Morlais Golf Club, Merthyr Tydfil   Dec 15

When first proposed at the local Macmillans committee, the idea of a lunch club was treated rather sceptically - not the kind of thing for a down to earth place like Merthyr. They could not have been more wrong. As you can see, not only was the Macmillan Ladies Luncheon Club a great social success with the ladies, more importantly through the social networks it facilitated, it proved vital to the fund raising effort for the Cancer Unit at the local Prince Charles hospital. That effort raised £1.2mn within 18 months and the chemotherapy unit started admitting patients from June 2010. With patients previously having to make the long, tiring and expensive trek to cancer treatment facilities in Cardiff 40 miles away, the project resonated strongly in the local community.

They Said It Couldn't Be Done in Merthyr   Morlais Golf Club, Merthyr Tydfil   Dec 15

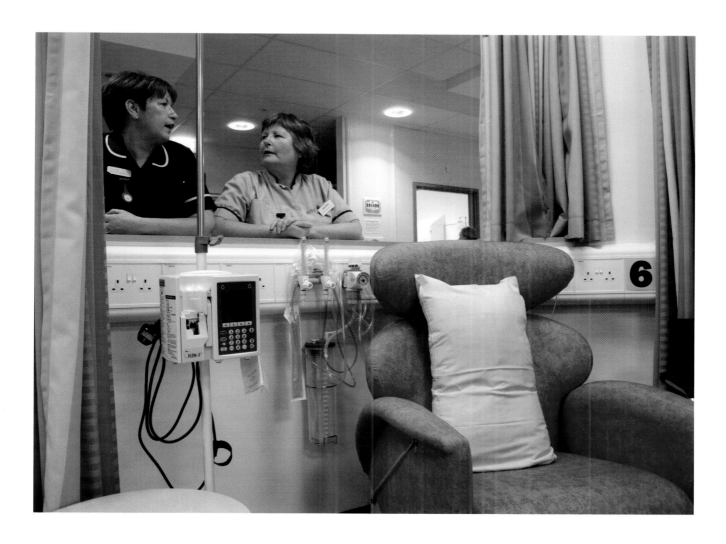

Chemotherapy   Prince Charles Hospital, Merthyr Tydfil   Dec 15

Constructed 1905-1907 at the height of the iron era, The Engine House fed a bank of towering Bessemer blast furnaces with air and was the hub of the Dowlais Iron Works.

The Next Tenant Was A Bulldozer   The Engine House, Dowlais, Merthyr Tydfil   Dec 15

A product of the Industrial Revolution, Merthyr Tydfil expanded from a modest village in the 1750s to be the largest town in Wales by 1801. The great Dowlais Works, then the largest iron works in the world, was the first to license the new steel manufacturing process from Henry Bessemer in 1856, following Bessemer's 1855 patent and after 9 years of R&D, steel was successfully produced in 1865 at Goat Mill, the world's most powerful steel rolling mill.

In 1899, Sir Ivor Guest sold the Dowlais works to

Arthur Keen who formed Guest, Keen & Co. Ltd. In 1902 Nettlefolds Ltd was acquired to create Guest, Keen and Nettlefolds, GKN , the large industrial concern that has lasted to the present day, capitalised in 2010 at c.£3bn.

However, after a period of prolonged decline, the production of steel at Dowlais finally came to an end in 1930. The mighty iron works has long since been demolished and all signs of it obliterated. Only the spoil tips on Merthyr Common on the horizon to the east testify to the huge scale of the iron industry in the Merthyr area.

As soon as Paul Marshallsea walked into the public viewing at the
Engine House in 2000, he decided: 'This place is going to be ours'.

Bloke Power   The Engine House, Dowlais, Merthyr Tydfil   Dec 15

During the 1990s, Paul, a local coal merchant in the Rhonda Valley, was
doing his bit refereeing football matches in the local Merthyr League and
running youth football teams, while his wife Wendy ran netball teams.
When their young son got involved in the local drugs and drink scene,
they became keenly aware of the high incidence of drug use amongst young
people in the area. The lack of local social facilities for young people was a
core issue - the kids wanted something to do, but just didn't have anywhere
to do it. It was clear they needed a place and the local authority, Merthyr
Tydfil Borough Council, didn't want to know. One local councillor stated:
'You'll never get this building up and running'.

Pant & Dowlais Boys and Girls Club   Dec 15

With its membership base in the Pant and Dowlais Boys and Girls Club, The Dowlais Blast Engine House Community Project opened in October 2005. Every night of the week, it now hosts 100-150 kids in a wide range of activities: football, netball, storytelling, cookery, music lessons, pool, art, computer games, digi training, dance, movies, gardening, environmental tidy ups etc etc.

The kids pay £1 upon entry and have a great place to play and meet, and the project has vastly improved the social health of the area. Anti Social Behaviour Orders are dramatically down and the youth make contact and form networks outside their school peer groups, ie outside traditional religious allegiances. Responsibility, fun and achievement are core values.

The Engine House sits on the site where steel was once rolled for the world.

Its present day Community Project should be rolled out nationally.

They Said It Couldn't Be Done in Merthyr   The Engine House, Dowlais, Merthyr Tydfil   Dec 15

In the project construction phase and as part of their social rehabilitation programme, being the lad that he is, Paul Marshallsea obtained the services of a few 'lifers' from the nearby Prescoed Open Prison - in fact they did quite a dangerous job in the roof space. When Prince Charles attended the opening ceremony in November 2005 (and since then being a great force for good behind the scenes in supporting the project), he was presented to one of these 'lifers' and asked: ' And where are you from ?' Apparently the unabashed Ronnie Williams replied : ' Well Sir, actually, I'm staying at one of your mother's places.'

Uniting the lyrical spirit of the Celtic Bards, the echo of the village chapel and the bonds of the working man, nothing could be more iconic in Wales than the Male Voice Choir - the mass crowd singing when Wales plays rugby in Cardiff is legendary. The love of song is a living tradition in Wales.

Locally based with a membership of about 60 and comprised of everyone from the postman to the chip shop proprietor, the Dowlais Male Voice Choir is a premier outfit with many fine recordings and top level performances all over Britain and Europe to its credit. The Choir's repertoire stretches from the sacred and secular through to traditional and classical music, including many pieces in the Welsh language. Here being put through its paces at one of its twice weekly rehearsals in Dowlais.

Dowlais Male Voice Choir   Dowlais, Merthyr Tydfil   Dec 15

The Sound Of The Valleys   Dowlais, Merthyr Tydfil   Dec 15

Considered a regicidal maniac by Monarchists for the execution of King Charles I, hated to his guts by the Irish for the dreadful massacres at Wexford and Drogheda, a hero for the Jews for rescinding Edward I's 366 year old expulsion order and a saviour of liberty to enlightenment thinkers, love him or loathe him and controversial he certainly was, nevertheless Oliver Cromwell was a pivotal figure in British history.

It is hard for us to imagine the incredible turmoil of the 1500s and 1600s - in modern terms, the massive systemic threat of the Cold War diced with the insidious street level terror post 9/11. On the political seismometer, the rupture with the Catholic Church in Britain, replicated across Europe in The Thirty Years War, was the World War II of its day - a historic event of immense proportions. Worse still, it set brother against brother, family against family, village against village, feudal lord against feudal lord and ultimately King against country. Add to that the medieval diet of plague, disease, poverty, hunger, tyranny and torture, and the everyday political atmos must have been like the soundtrack of an Alfred Hitchcock thriller.

On the rock bottom core point, his passionate opposition to papal and clerical authority as against the primacy of the Bible, at root the primacy of spirituality over organised religion, Oliver Cromwell just about had history and justice on his side. The contradictions of Oliver Cromwell, the struggle between fanatical idealism and ruthless realpolitik, were epitomized in such comments of his as : 'Necessity has no law.' 'Put your trust in God, but keep your powder dry' and his oft quoted comment on the King's execution : 'a cruel necessity.'

From unlikely beginnings in the middle gentry in Huntingdon and as MP for Cambridge, Cromwell excelled as a military commander in the Civil War, rapidly rising to become Lieutenant-General of Cavalry in 1645, second-in-command of the New Model Army under Sir Thomas Fairfax. This ensured he was at the heart of events leading up to the execution of Charles I, the abolition of the Monarchy and the House of Lords, the ensuing Parliamentary based government and the Council of State of The Commonwealth from 1649 to 1653.

Beast Or Saviour - Oliver Cromwell   House of Commons, Westminster, London   Dec 16

Instrument Of Government - Dec 16, 1653

The Instrument of Government of 1653, together with the later document of 1657, the Humble Petition and Advice, was Britain's first, and last, attempt at a written constitution. A not unreasonable stab at a separation of powers between an Executive, a Council of State with 13-21 members and a triennial Parliament with 460 MPs. Oliver Cromwell became its first Lord Protector, Executive, on December 16, 1653.

As decreed in the Instrument, free elections were held in June 1654 and 460 MPs duly assembled in the First Protectorate Parliament in September 1654. Cromwell and the Council of State had high hopes for the incoming Parliament and presented 82 Ordinances ranging from financial, legal and religious reforms to highway repair and traffic regulations in London. But the House included presbyterians, republicans and royalist sympathisers, hostile to the Protectorate and resentful of the continuing political influence of the Army. Amidst incessant bickering and 'bird witted opinionators', the Parliament did not even pass one of the Ordinances. So, in January 1654, an angered and frustrated Cromwell dissolved the Parliament at the first constitutional opportunity.

If the Taliban wish to improve their social control techniques, they could do worse than study the Puritan regime of Britain in the 1650s. The infamous Rule of the Major Generals shut down many inns and theatres, forbad swearing and horse racing, whipped boys that played football on Sundays, banned colourful make up and licentious dressing for women and enforced a fast day once a month.

Needless to say, in such a human place as Britain, it was to be the first and last attempt at being compelled to obey the commandment : 'Thou Shalt Be Good '. Ever since then, the word 'Puritan' has been embedded within British culture as a derogatory term for moralisers of all kinds. Nor is this healthy disrespect for 'holier than thou' types confined to Christianity. As the Pakistani taxi driver in Manchester put it : 'The first one in the mosque is the most dishonest'.

The other legacy is that Britain tore up the rule book on having a written constitution - that privilege would be left to the Puritan experiment on the other side of the Atlantic. As for constitutional issues since then, well, Britain has just riffed it.

The Part Of Ireland That Is Britain   Newtownards Road, East Belfast   Dec 22

In the early 1900s, Belfast was a thriving industrial city with a population of around 390,000 and many of its citizens were employed in the linen, engineering and shipbuilding industries. Harland & Wolff, the largest of these shipyards, built over 70 vessels for the White Star Line, the most famous of these being the Olympic Class vessels : Olympic, Titanic and Britannic, designed and built between 1908 and 1914. The Titanic departed its final fit in Belfast on April 2nd 1912 and sailed from Southampton on April 10th. It struck the iceberg five days later on April 14th 1912 with the loss of 1,523 lives.

After 142 years of world class shipbuilding, the last ship to be built by Harland & Wolff was Ship No: 1742, the 20,000 ton 'Anvil Point', launched in April 2003. Now part of the Norwegian offshore engineering company Fred Olsen Energy, Harland & Wolff employs c. 500 people mainly in offshore wind power technology. Short Brothers, the specialist aircraft company and a subsidiary of Canadian Bombardier Aerospace is the largest manufacturing concern in present day Northern Ireland with c. 5,300 employees.

Christmas Shopping   Victoria Square Shopping Mall, Belfast   Dec 22

The Part Of Britain That Is Ireland

Falls Road, Belfast

Sean Maguire, 'The Maestro', one of the greatest exponents of traditional Irish music was born into a Belfast musical family and played the fiddle since he was 12-years-old. He famously turned down an invitation to join the Belfast Symphony Orchestra because he felt more at home playing traditional music. "I decided to devote my techniques to the furtherance and promotion of my culture " In 1949 at the age of only twenty-one, he won the Oireachtas, the All-Ireland musical championship held annually in Dublin, with the only perfect score ever awarded in the long history of the competition. He went on from there to enjoy an illustrious performance career all over the world.

The Belfast man rewrote the book on fiddle playing with a combination of dazzling virtuosity, high creativity and passion for performance. With the advantage of classical training, it was a style which pushed the boundaries, nettled the fundamentalists and which he himself called 'progressive traditional' : 'I explored all the possibilities to transform the tunes by arranging, key changes, different bow stylings, and not so much the "rumpy tumpy" style of playing Irish music.' 'The music was in a primitive state. The Irish had been denied their culture for so long by the English occupation ; not being allowed to play, sing, or speak the language, and all go together. Read the history of our country, and you know why the music, like our language, nearly disappeared. Now its all coming back.... there is no danger now that it will ever go back to being primitive.'

Sean Maguire recalled a typical Irish Ceili of his youth :

' The kitchen was got ready; it was at a person's house. It was made spotless, flagstone floors. There would be the turf stacked to keep the fire burning. The porter or Guinness would be ready to hand, and anybody that wanted to partake of the beverage, they could help themselves. The smell of home-baked bread; you just couldn't wait to get it! And meanwhile the merry-making went on. You were called on to play a solo, play a few tunes, sing a few songs. The balladeer was always there.

But one feature of the Irish ceili was the story teller, he was a character in his own right. He told more lies than were ever published, but it was all in good fun! Then there would be dancing; someone would be called on to dance a step. And that was in real boots; it sounded like a corps of drummers on that flagstone floor. Those dancers were genuine experts! But I loved the Sean Nós singing, the old unaccompanied traditional singing. It was gorgeous, and believe me it drew you very near to nature.

And a stranger was always welcome. No questions were ever asked. If you came in and wanted to be part of the night's enjoyment, you were made welcome. It started at eight or nine oclock, and went on till five in the morning. And many's the summer morning, somebody would say, sitting by the window ; the blinds would have been drawn for the night; "Whats that blue light there?" It was daylight! They had played, and danced, and sung all night.'

The Dark Stuff   The Morning Star, Pottinger's Entry, Belfast   Dec 22

Winter Fells   Keswick, Cumbria   Dec 24

Loweswater   Lake District, Cumbria   Dec 24

When, in climate change decades to come, the good citizens of Gateshead and Berwick on Tweed are slapping on factor 35 sunscreen on Christmas Day, these scenes will doubtless seem quaint.

In fact, Britain had the coldest December since records began. Many places recorded their lowest ever temperatures and the average temperature for the month was minus 1C . Although globally, the world had one of its warmest years, in Britain overall, 2010 was the 12th coldest year since 1910.

Frozen Motion   Buttermere, Cumbria   Dec 24

Ice Age   Buttermere, Cumbria   Dec 24

The Lady From The Forest   Trafalgar Square, London   Dec 16

Each year since 1947, a Christmas tree has been given to the people of London from the people of Norway in gratitude for Britain's support for Norway during World War II . Usually a Norwegian spruce, *Picea Albes*, over 20 metres high and 50-60 years old, a regal specimen is selected from the forests around Oslo with great care several months, even years in advance. The tree is felled in November during a ceremony in which the Lord Mayor of Westminster, the British Ambassador to Norway and the Mayor of Oslo participate. A specialist rigging team erects the tree in Trafalgar Square using a hydraulic crane and it is decorated in traditional Norwegian fashion, with vertical strings of lights. Energy efficient light bulbs are now used and after Christmas, the tree is taken down and recycled into mulch.

A full programme of carol singing takes place under the tree each evening for the two weeks before Christmas. On this occasion, the Great Gustos sing for the St George's Hospital Charity.

Neighbourhood   Bowdon, Cheshire   Dec 24

Ever since Mrs Ludlow started it in 1959, the Christmas Eve neighbourhood carol singing has taken place every year on the same street corner in Bowdon. After she left the area in 1977, it was taken over by Rod Chadwick (centre in hat) who has organized it on the last 34 occasions. In ice rink conditions and as usual in aid of the NSPCC, the 2010 collection raised £190 for this very good cause.

The Cheshire Hunt   Tarporley, Cheshire   **Dec 27**

Horses And Hounds   Tarporley, Cheshire   Dec 27

3 - 2 - 1   Hogmanay, Edinburgh   New Year's Eve

This Is Us   Hogmanay, Edinburgh   New Year's Eve

etcetera

when a famous person enters a room people turn their heads
and momentarily stop doing whatever they were doing

when a camera enters a space
people put on an imaginary face and reality is arrested
or there is an element of self consciousness
a tell tale tension in the body language

the observing part of our nature wants to see
a football crowd watching a football match
not football supporters reacting to images of themselves
on the stadium big screen

we all want reality to be real

because of this
within the boundaries of good taste and common sense
the documentary maker has limited rights to observe reality as it is
so that we may more accurately be aware of ourselves

it is in this spirit
that this work has been submitted
to tell the story of a Britain as it is

we gratefully acknowledge and thank
all the people and organisations that have contributed to this work
we trust that their images have been depicted
in a fair and reasonable way

any alterations of images have been kept to an absolute minimum
mainly to restore the original quality of a scene
a blue sky was reinstated in New Year Posh
and yes the sky was as blue as that in Palazzo at Blenheim Palace
overall the year was blessed with well above average fine weather

as for Britain itself
there is much to do
and many challenges in the years ahead
even so perhaps this work might show
that Britain is a more interesting
a more inspiring place
than we might otherwise have thought

a documentary work

Textures
a set of 8 greetings cards

Mesmeric

Dawn

Earth

Ocean

Meadow

Moors

Forest

Wheatfield

123 x 170mm
blank inside

8 cards with envelopes - £4.00

order online

www.inspirita.org

Season's greetings
a set of 8 greetings cards

Loweswater

Winter Oak

123 x 170mm
season's greetings inside

8 cards with envelopes - £3.00
4 of each card

order online

other documentary works

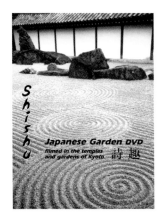

'Shishu'
Japanese Garden Culture
DVD 53mins

'The Unchanging Self'
Indian Spiritual Culture
DVD 67mins

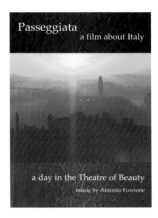

'Passeggiata'
a film about Italy
DVD 70mins

'Sfakia'
Greek Island Life
DVD 72mins

'The Heart Of Today'
a film about New York
DVD 124mins

'God, Chocolate & The Black Stars'
a moment in Africa
DVD 49mins

www.inspirita.org